WRITE WHAT YOU HAVE SEEN

DAVE HINKLE

"Write, therefore, what you have seen,
what is now and what will take place later."

Revelation 1:19

Write What You Have Seen

Trilogy Christian Publishers A Wholly Owned Subsidiary of Trinity Broadcasting Network
2442 Michelle Drive Tustin, CA 92780

Cover design by: Kelly Stewart
For information about special discounts for bulk purchases, please contact Trilogy Christian Publishing.
Manufactured in the United States of America
10 9 8 7 6 5 4 3 2 1
Library of Congress Cataloging-in-Publication Data is available.
ISBN: 978-1-68556-727-9
E-ISBN: 978-1-68556-728-6

DEDICATED TO THE NEXT GENERATION

Olivia, Jackson, Emory, Asa, and the Peanuts

I love you so much!

"I have no greater joy than to hear my children are walking in the truth."

3 John 1:4

CONTENTS

PREFACE

As a teenager, the Apostle John traveled with Jesus. The Bible tells us he was one of Christ's closest friends. He was referred to as "the one whom Jesus loved." John, a pillar of the early Christian church, wrote five books of the New Testament. Later in life, John was exiled to the Greek Isle of Patmos for professing his faith. While there, John, hearing directly from God, then wrote the prophetic book of Revelation. His initial instructions from God:

> "Write, therefore, what you have seen,
> what is now and what will take place later."
>
> Revelation 1:19

John is a hero of mine, but I am not John. This is not prophecy. This is not Revelation. God did not speak to me in a dream, vision, or audible voice. Some of this book is not even serious! I am, however, inspired by this verse and I do feel called to write what I have seen—good, bad, indifferent, inspired, humorous, or sad. I have tried my best to follow that calling by recounting inspiring stories of God's work in the lives of everyday people. The results of His work are exactly what you will read in the pages ahead.

INTRODUCTION

As a college freshman in 1978, our English professor returned my composition by slapping it on the desk. He then sneered, "Son, I don't know what you'll grow up to be, but it certainly won't be a writer!" His comments did not phase me in the least because I had never once considered being a writer. I thought I would just chalk that off my list of potential careers, which I did—for seventeen years. That all changed in 1995 when I was tapped on the shoulder by my friend, retired USAF Colonel Don Waddell. His firm, military approach and words of direction still ring in my ears. "Dave, I'm too busy this week to write my newspaper column, so you will." He never paid a second of attention to my objections as he walked off.

Writing a column for the first time ever and substituting for a very popular columnist was a daunting task. But not wanting to disappoint the Colonel, I got busy. I have zero memory of the content of that column, nor do I have a copy, but I do know it was miraculously published. Nonetheless, my occasional columns continued until I eventually alternated weeks with Don. Don and the editor took me under their wings and honed my skills, sometimes firmly, as I continued perfecting my craft. I wrote, off and on, for that newspaper for over twenty years. Some of those stories appear in this book. I will be forever grateful to my great friend Don, my trusted writing advisor, Ruth Schenk, and Esther Jaggers, who provided many leads for my initial writing platform, the Southeast Christian Outlook.

As I have matured as a writer, I like to believe that I have also matured in my walk with the Lord. I really can't describe exactly what has happened, but if you knew me then and know me now, you would be amazed too at what the Lord has done with me. Maybe the people I write about rub off on me. I'm still incredibly imperfect, but I am grateful the past is gone, and I am excited about the future. I am also very grateful for one of God's powerful instruments, Southeast Christian Church in Louisville, KY. I could tell you a hundred stories of how God has worked, in amazing ways, through this church, and maybe I will someday.

For now, let me just say one word—grace.

The amazing grace of our Lord and Savior Jesus Christ is indeed amazing. There is abundant grace for you, me, and everyone. Retired Southeast Senior Minister Bob Russell taught grace superbly in his sermons. I never understood grace before 1995. I do now. Thank you, Southeast. Thank you, Bob. Hopefully, that grace is evident in the pages of this book. And thanks to my siblings, Allen, B, Cara, Jo, Mo, and Annie, as well as cousins Bobbie and Bennie, who have all shown and taught me grace. I love you all dearly. As for the title of this book, I credit my friend and Christian brother, Scott Kippes, who, knowing my love for writing, crafted me a personalized wooden cross bearing that handwritten scripture. So, I chose that verse as the book title. I treasure his gift as I treasure the folks in this book.

This book is a collection of my favorite stories over the past twenty years, the result of encounters, observations, interviews, and writing. They are about real people, old friends and new, who share their stories with joy, tears, laughter, and transparency. They are stories about changed lives and of those changing lives. They are stories of family, inspiration, and adventurous roads I have traveled. But the stories are primarily about changed lives, stories designed to enlighten and inspire, stories such as Peggy and Winston Bennett. Their journey is perhaps the most amazing I have ever heard of, let alone written. Each chapter is of a changed life or of one changing lives. Either way, it is ultimately the Lord's work, not theirs or mine. My prayer is that you enjoy and are touched by their stories. Hopefully, I, like John in Revelation, will be a faithful scribe for the Lord.

Turn the Page and Read
Things You Should Know About Me
Before Reading This Book

I AM CRAZY

I believe in an invisible God who created the universe. I believe His Son, Jesus Christ, lived a perfect life on this earth and was crucified for our sin. I believe He was raised from the dead, went to heaven, and will return some day. I believe His Spirit now lives within me. I am crazy.

I believe in the Bible as the perfect, unerring Word of God. I believe God speaks to us through His Word. I believe the Bible has all answers for living a successful, fulfilling, rewarding and purposeful life. I believe in the incredible number of Old Testament prophecies that foretold the story of Jesus Christ. I am crazy.

I believe a man named Jonah lived three days in the belly of a whale. I believe in a flood that covered the earth. I believe in the virgin birth. I believe a donkey once spoke to a man. I believe in Adam, Eve, Noah, Abraham, Moses, Ruth, David, Mary, Matthew, Mark, Luke, John, Peter, Paul, and all the other biblical heroes. I believe they once walked the earth. I believe their stories. I believe every word in the Bible. I am crazy.

I believe in Satan, evil, sin, and eternal consequences. I believe in a place called hell. I believe I sin every day, but

I also believe in salvation by grace and faith, not by works. I believe Jesus' resurrection is the single most important event in the history of the world. I am crazy.

I believe in renewal by baptism. I believe in the personal transforming power of Jesus Christ. I have seen it. I believe He can change lives forever. I believe He changed mine. I talk to Him every day. He talks to me. I am crazy.

I am crazy for writing this. I am crazy for believing these things. I believe in mental guidance that comes from the Holy Spirit. I believe God puts people in our path for fulfilling His plans. I believe He often speaks through songs and nature. I believe I can recognize Him in others and that He speaks to me through them. I am crazy.

I believe He shows Himself in men and women of great power, wealth, and notoriety. I believe He shows Himself in the unnoticed, lowly, and weak. I believe He is a stern but loving God. I believe His ways are mysterious and mostly misunderstood. I believe His presence is often found strongest in battlefields, cancer wards, and funeral homes. I believe He spares some from death but not others. I cannot fathom why. But I still believe. I am crazy.

I believe in love, far beyond my understanding. I believe in the power found in humility. I believe He loves me despite what I have done in the past. I believe He will use this book for good, if even for one person. I believe despite my feelings. I believe in forgiveness, even when it hurts. I believe in the impossible. I am crazy.

I believe even though I cannot see Him. I believe He will use my ears, mouth, eyes, and hands for His purposes. I believe He infuses me with energy, power, peace, joy, and contentment—despite the circumstances. I believe in blessings and miracles far beyond my comprehension. I'm okay with being a Jesus freak. I am crazy.

I believe He knows my heart, mind, and DNA. I believe He created me. I do not believe in evolution and other gods. I do not place my trust in money, possessions, or popularity. I place my trust in the Lord Jesus Christ. I believe in the Ten Commandments and every miracle He performed, including those in my life. I am crazy.

I believe in the men and women He has placed in my life to aid, assist, rebuke, and empower me. I believe in the power of prayer. I believe even when my prayers are not answered my way. I trust He has a great plan for me. I trust when I have no apparent reason to do so. I trust in other crazy people. I am crazy.

I believe God is serious about His business. I believe

He expects us to love Him with all our heart, love our neighbors, and go make disciples. I believe His commandments are complex yet simple. I believe a ten-year-old can understand and obey the Gospel. I believe that, like a good shepherd, Jesus will guard and protect his flock and that He will welcome them back, no matter how far they have strayed. I believe this incredible, unseen force is the consummate Teacher, Counselor, Prince of Peace, Lord and Savior. I am crazy.

I believe Jesus lived on earth and was crucified for our sin and for our salvation. I believe Him to be the only person in the history of the world to come back from death and return to heaven. I believe someday He will return to earth in power and majesty. I believe every knee shall bow, and I believe He will take his chosen ones to heaven. If I do not experience this event, I will die someday soon and be taken to a perfect eternity to be with Him and those chosen ones who have gone on before.

I believe every word I just wrote.

I believe I am crazy.

CHANGED LIVES, CHANGING LIVES

> "Listen, I tell you a mystery; we will not all sleep, but we all will be changed."
>
> 1 Corinthians 15:51

I find this section about change perhaps the most meaningful of the book because the people are so fascinating, as is change itself. Change is continual and all around us. We are forced to deal with changes in our health, occupation, church, address, family, friends, favorite sports teams, and so much more. Change is inevitable, unavoidable, and often necessary. Yet, few will embrace change or welcome it. Most of us even strongly resist it. We like our comfort zones. We try to avoid change, but nonetheless, there in our face, constantly, is our mental foe—change.

Change can be good, or change can be bad. Change can be easy or extraordinarily difficult, quick or slow, minor or dramatic. The stories you will read here are often of radical change and change that usually occurs "between the ears and in the heart," not circumstantially driven. Some of the people you will meet in these chapters have had their lives forever changed by being rescued from sexual addiction, alcoholism, drugs, pride, indifference, and a host of other life-destroying crises. Some of their names have been changed for protective reasons, but they are all real people, and their stories are very true. Others you will meet here are changing lives, helping others through kindness, persistence, prayer, service, humility, and love. I salute both the changed lives and the change-makers. They have my utmost respect and admiration. They have inspired and changed me. For that, I am incredibly grateful.

Obviously, my love changed lives. In examining their stories, I often find myself searching for the common denominator of what created the change. In some cases, change occurs from sheer self-determination or "white-knuckling," as some refer to it. But in my experience and observation, that approach rarely works, certainly not long term. The only true cure I have concluded is the powerful, mysterious, wonderful, long-lasting, amazing, and joyful redemptive power of Jesus Christ. May you and I find that and our own change in the inspirational stories on the pages ahead.

Shapley, Jason, Judy & Shap

Lucky Jason

"Surely You have granted him eternal blessings and made him glad, with the joy of Your presence."

Psalm 21:6

Jason was indeed lucky. He was born in 1979 to a wonderful, loving, Christian woman, Judy. Ten years later, he would have a devoted Christian stepfather, Shap, and half-brother, Shapley. Jason was cared for and provided for in fine fashion. He had the love, respect, and admiration of countless family and friends. Jason was blessed greatly. His family was determined to show Jason the world. So, together, they explored the United States, Mexico, Jamaica, the Dominican Republic, St. Lucia, Antigua, Barbados, the British Virgin Islands, Canada, Italy, Croatia, Greece, Slovenia, Turkey, Great Britain, Scotland, Ireland, Netherlands, Belgium, France and took several cruise ship adventures. But there's much more to Jason's story.

Jason was born six weeks early—dead but revived. His seventeen-year-old mother knew the situation was grim, but she had little clue what was ahead. Judy was in the midst of a very difficult marriage that would end in divorce. Now, she had an even bigger challenge.

Jason was diagnosed as a spastic quadriplegic with cerebral palsy. He had meningitis and scoliosis that made his back arch. He was given five years to live, at the most. He never walked or talked. He had a feeding tube. He wore diapers his entire life. He spent his first eighteen years in and out of hospitals where the family often celebrated holidays, birthdays, and anniversaries. Jason endured a body cast, spinal fusions, bed sores, frequent bouts with pneumonia, infections, skin grafts, and countless surgeries. Judy was told many times that Jason would not survive. But Judy never let ominous news deter her resolve to take care of Jason. One surgery lasted seventeen hours. After surgery, the exhausted surgeon told Judy, "There is only one reason Jason is alive—the love you have given him."

Jason was lucky because his family gave him every ounce of love and energy they had. Judy spent the better part of thirty-two years caring for Jason around the clock. Feeding Jason often took three hours as he could only intake very slowly, and Jason ate three times a day. Judy embraced her responsibilities, and her love for Jason never faded.

Jason was also lucky because when he was ten years old, Shap arrived on the scene. Shap and Judy met on a blind date. When their relationship blossomed, friends pulled Shap aside and asked him about Jason. Shap simply replied, "It doesn't bother me." Two years later, in 1991, Judy and Shap were married. Shap was asked why he would marry into such a situation. His response was, "Marry into this family? Why not? I love Judy. I loved Jason. They needed me. I needed them. Unless you are scared of taking on responsibility, why not? It's really pretty simple."

During hospital stays, Shap would plan weekend jaunts for the family. They took Jason sightseeing, to state parks, and to various places of interest—anywhere Shap could find to entertain Jason and give the family a respite from hospital life. Those regional, Midwest trips would set the stage for world travel.

By the time Jason was eighteen, his health had stabilized to the point he could venture far beyond home and hospitals. Judy and Shap had big plans, and they were not to be deterred by Jason's physical condition. Ultimately, those plans took them to over twenty countries.

Perhaps their greatest memories were of the people they encountered around the world. Judy and Shap say people were attracted to Jason and his infectious smile. They were constantly stopped by those who wanted to interact with Jason and hear his story. Clergy and nuns took a keen interest in Jason. They prayed over him and the family and would give Jason various religious mementos. On return trips to previously visited locales, Judy and Shap were amazed at the number of times they were excitedly approached by people who remembered Jason. Evidently, Jason blessed people everywhere he went.

Jason was also lucky to have his brother Shapley. Judy and Shap agree that Shapley understood Jason, was very good with him and did not shy away from helping with Jason's needs. Shapley was given, by his school, a standing ovation when receiving a distinguished award for service to his brother. Shapley now has a son whose middle name is Jason.

At the age of thirty-two, in 2011, Jason became even more lucky when he passed painlessly and peacefully, from his mother's arms to the arms of Jesus. Judy recalls, "Jason did not talk, but he clearly communicated through his smile, eyes, cough, and expressions. That's how he touched so many people both here and in our travels. He had a greater impact on people than we will ever know. Jesus has been with us every single day. We always knew

Jason was being watched over. Jason is still blessing people, and Jesus is still blessing us. I'm sad Jason's gone. He left ten years ago, and it still hurts, but we know he is well taken care of."

"Even during those thirty-two years, I never felt sorry for myself because God won't give you anything that He won't help you with. I was chosen because He knew I could handle it. I can't really be sad because Jason is now getting to do things that he couldn't do here on earth. For me to be angry would be selfish. His final trip was to heaven. Now he is like any other healthy man. He was as abnormal as he could be but to me, he was as normal as he could be. Jason was here for a reason, and I was a part of the reason. I was lucky to be Jason's mom."

Peggy and Winston Bennett

Sexual Addiction

> "Therefore, confess your sins to each other and pray for each other so that you may be healed. The prayer of a righteous person is powerful and effective."
>
> James 5:16

If a husband had hundreds of extramarital affairs over the course of fifteen years, why would his wife stay? Peggy Bennett said, "It's all about Jesus Christ." Her husband, Winston Bennett, is, by his own admission, a sexual addict. "To say I had hundreds of encounters with other women is not an exaggeration," Winston said. "Sex was Winston's drug of choice," Peggy added. Winston was a star at every level of basketball—high school, college, and professional. After a stellar career at Louisville's Male High School, Winston went on to become an All-SEC forward at the University of Kentucky, where he played for Hall of Fame coaches Joe B. Hall and Eddie Sutton.

Winston then played professionally for the Cleveland Cavaliers and Miami Heat before ending his career playing in Europe. During his athletic career, Winston played alongside many Hall of Fame NBA players, such as Larry Bird, Magic Johnson, and Charles Barkley. Following his playing career, Winston served as an assistant coach for the UK and then for the Boston Celtics. Both coaching roles were under the guidance of one of his mentors, Rick Pitino.

Ultimately, Winston lost his dream job with the Celtics and left Boston in disgrace because of sexual misconduct. Winston said his fall from stardom caused him to lose dignity, money, and reputation. Along the basketball trail, Winston apparently had plenty of opportunity for sexual encounters with females who undoubtedly were attracted to the famous six-foot-seven-inch handsome basketball star. But basketball is only one aspect of the Bennett story that has unfolded over the course of their twenty-three-year marriage. Why did Peggy stay?

She said she was initially very resistant to even the thought of forgiveness. She said she prayed, "'God, is this what you want me to do? Stay?' I knew what God says about adultery and divorce, so I prayed hard, and every time I did, God told me to love him, forgive him, and trust Him. It was difficult for me to accept. I could not imagine what kind of God would ask for this. But God knew Winston's heart, a heart that was crying out for help."

According to Peggy, Winston was trapped in a stronghold of Satan. Winston said he had known, since his youth, the truth of the Bible. He said that knowledge would cause tremendous guilt and shame after each encounter, yet he always returned to his addiction. Peggy said she began to view Winston's predicament as a disease. She said, "Yes, it's very ugly, but if he had terminal cancer, would I walk away?" So, Peggy slowly began to feel that it was meant for her to walk this journey and that she would have to learn to love Winston as God does. She confidently stated, "If I didn't respond in God's way, this would not have worked."

Peggy began a prayer journey that she said has lasted more than ten years—and even to this day. While Winston continually tried and failed, Peggy prayed, endured, and focused on love and forgiveness. Winston said he understands that addicts are never completely cured, but he also said that he has been clean for five years, "Everything said about this story is true," he said. "I am not proud of my behavior. I pray for healing for the pain I have caused my family and the women I hurt. I was finally able to break my addiction but only through the prayers of my wife. I love my wife so much for what she has done for me and our family, but it's not about us. It's about our Lord and Savior, Jesus Christ."

Peggy is passionate about explaining what God has done for her family, and they now speak publicly about their journey. They shared their testimony on ESPN when Winston was a head basketball coach at Mid-Continent University in Mayfield, KY—a far cry from the NBA. "If not for the Lord's grace and mercy, we both know we would not be married today," she said. "I am in awe of what he has done for us individually and in our marriage. The last eight years have been the best of our lives."

Peggy and Winston have endured a great deal in the process of pain, loss, and public humiliation. Peggy puts it all in perspective. "Look what Jesus has done for all of us," she said. "Who are we to say we won't go through pain. We are to be like Him, even in suffering. Every day I give Him glory and honor for what He has done for us."

Dr. Russell Ries

More Than a Surgeon

> "In the same way, good deeds are obvious, and even those that are not obvious cannot remain hidden forever."
>
> 1 Timothy 5:25

I stood in the corner of a busy operating room, hoping no one would notice me. Medical professionals scurried about preparing a patient for a surgical procedure. Residents, nurses, and an anesthesiologist all awaited the arrival of the star of the show. In his trademark humility, he would never want to be known as a star. But he was. Dr. Russell Ries entered the room. He calmly surveyed the patient, politely asked for an instrument, and confidently began his specialty—facial plastic surgery. After a few minutes, without even a pause, he said, with a laugh, "Dave, you can't see anything from over there. Stand on this stool, so you can look over my shoulder and see the procedure up close." He didn't have to do that. But he did. He didn't have to invite me into his operating room. But he did. He didn't have to teach me how to properly dress for the OR. But he did. He didn't have to calm my nerves with his classic humor. But he did.

As a rookie surgical consultant, I was learning my own craft. My job was to develop relationships with key craniofacial surgeons, demonstrate the benefits of my company's products for facial reconstruction, and consult in the OR. Dr. Ries not only became a champion of our brand but also introduced me to his colleagues around the country. He didn't have to do that. But he did.

Perhaps my favorite memories of Dr. Ries were the times spent in his office. He invited me in one afternoon to enjoy what would become frequent visits. Just the two of us would drink coffee and talk about life. He would proudly show me the latest addition to his colorful facial mask collection on his office wall. He would, with a smile on his face, tell me all about his family. He would show a genuine interest in my life. He didn't have to do that. But he did.

I attended many medical conferences in various major cities with Dr. Ries. He made sure I had an invitation to dinner with his colleagues. We ate well, we laughed and had much fun. He asked me to call him Russell. But I never did. I just had too much respect for him. He had taken me under his wing. Maybe he was partial to me. Maybe he was partial to many others. I suspect he was. That would be like him. He didn't have to do that. But he did.

After my medical consulting days ended, our

friendship did not. I kept his cell phone number and am very glad I did. Occasionally, I would call him for a quick, friendly chat. Once again, he always made time for me, especially when situations were urgent. When my niece was critically injured in a car accident, he took my call. He met the Life Flight helicopter personally, assessed the situation, made all necessary arrangements then performed successful facial reconstructive surgery. He comforted her mother, my sister. He compassionately worked with us for months in my niece's rehabilitation. He didn't have to do that. But he did.

On two other separate occasions, close friends of mine faced dire medical situations. Both times, Dr. Ries answered my call. Though neither case was his specialty, he utilized his network to quickly connect my friends with first-class care. He followed up. He met for discussions at the hospital. He cared. He didn't have to do that. But he did.

I was shocked and deeply saddened upon hearing of his death. I read his obituary in disbelief. I shed tears. He was my friend.

I've worked with many surgeons across the country, but none like Dr. Ries. He loved Jesus Christ. He loved his family. He had impeccable integrity and character. He was kind, humble, considerate, generous, professional, funny, talented, trustworthy, helpful, friendly, devoted, successful, skilled, caring, compassionate, loyal, hard-working, dedicated, and always accessible. He didn't have to do all that. But he did.

Dr. Ries went to heaven in 2021.
To the Ries family,
may the Peace of Christ be with you.

Mamaw

Mamaw

> "Charm is deceptive, and beauty is fleeting;
> but a woman who fears the Lord is to be praised."
>
> Proverbs 31:30

Rob Greenrose got the call no one wants. His ninety-seven-year-old grandmother called and said, "Rob, I don't feel well. I think I'm dying." Rob rushed to Mamaw's home. While waiting for assistance to arrive, he sat on the edge of her bed and held her hand as she began talking about the past. "I miss your Papaw. I miss Charlie and all my brothers and sisters," she said. "Mamaw, if you want to go home to be with Jesus and your family, it's okay. We will be fine," Rob replied. With that, Mamaw smiled and took her last breath.

Rob's grandparents, Don (Papaw) and Amanda Terry (Mamaw), and his Uncle Charlie played a hugely formative role in his life. As a child, he spent summers at his grandparents' farm. "It was a simple life," Rob said. "I got away from everything else. We had horses, cattle, and a garden. The men worked the farm. Mamaw took care of her men and served everyone. Those were the best times ever." Mamaw took her grandson to church and set a firm spiritual standard. "I remember every night after the men went to bed, Mamaw would pull out her Bible, writing journal, and study materials to spend time with her Lord," Rob added. "I will never forget that or her. I loved her, and I miss her."

Rob also learned practical examples of faith. "On that farm, I learned how much God loves us," he added. "Papaw loved his family, and he loved his farm. If one animal strayed away, he would rescue it. He always took great care of those animals. I now know Papaw's love and care for his family and farm is an incredible example of how God loves us, cares for us, and brings us back when we stray." Rob's wife of thirty years, Susan, also held Mamaw in high regard. "She was an amazing woman," she said. "She knew the Bible inside and out. She was a humble prayer warrior who had an intimate relationship with Jesus Christ." Charlie (always known as just Charlie, not Uncle Charlie) also taught Rob life lessons. "Charlie never left the farm his entire life, but he was very smart," he said. "He was a hard worker. He, too, took great pride in the family, the farm, the garden, and the animals. He taught me love for family. He taught me work ethic. We were very close."

Last phone calls have been a pattern for Rob, whose

grandfather and uncle died many years prior to Mamaw. "Papaw called me and asked me to come see him, but I was too busy with my friends," Rob said. "He died the next day, and I was crushed. I thought I would never get over not going to see him." Later, when Charlie became seriously ill, he too called Rob. "I rushed to the hospital where he told me he just wanted to go home to the farm and die," he said. "I considered it and could have done it, but I didn't.

Charlie died soon after, and I never thought I would get over not granting Charlie his last wish." Being with Mamaw as she died helped Rob forgive himself for not fulfilling the final wishes of his grandfather and uncle. Finally, he had been at the right place at the right time to say goodbye. After those summers at the farm, Rob became a U.S. Army Ranger. He later built a successful business. He and Susan have two children and a new granddaughter. Through five generations, there seems to be one constant, Jesus Christ. Papaw and Charlie would be proud. So would Mamaw.

James

James

> "James, a servant of God and of the Lord Jesus Christ, To the twelve tribes scattered among the nations: Greetings."
>
> James 1:1

New Testament writer James, the brother of Jesus, was a prominent, influential, and respected leader of first-century Christians. He was an elder of the church in Jerusalem. The Apostle Paul referred to James as a pillar of the church. James' writings were focused on encouraging Christian Jews living outside of Israel, and his book is often referred to as a down-to-earth, practical daily guide for Christian living.

Twenty centuries later, James' teachings were brought to life by Alvin Price of Louisville, Kentucky, when he began replicating, from memory, the exact words of the book of James. Alvin, wearing authentic first-century attire, has now recited, in dramatic fashion, the entire book of James in over two hundred dramas over the course of eighteen years.

Alvin, now eighty, still performs his drama, but he remembers his original calling, "I was teaching an adult

Bible class on the book of James, and it occurred to me that memorizing those five chapters would be very meaningful. So, I challenged the class to memorize along with me. I was the only one to do so! I knew it would be good for me, and it was. It took me about three months, but I did it. Shortly thereafter, I was cast in the role of Nicodemus in our church Easter production.

When I realized that God had given me a gift for acting, I told Him, "Lord, if you will enable me to turn the book of James into a dramatic presentation, I'll take it wherever you want—wherever you open the doors. And that is what I've done, from Kentucky to Michigan to Florida to Texas and places in between." Alvin has reached audiences ranging from two to eight hundred in churches, prisons, schools, videos, and many others. Alvin never charges for his drama, rarely turns down invitations, and pays his own travel expenses. He does accept gifts. He says they range from a few dollars to very generous. He said, "I don't do this for money. The Lord has always provided."

Dr. David R. Reagan is the founder of Lamb & Lion Ministries and is considered by many an international Bible prophecy expert. Reagan had this to say, "When I first experienced Alvin Price's dramatic presentation of the book of James, I was so emotionally and spiritually impacted by it that I decided to invite him to come to the headquarters of Lamb & Lion Ministries in Dallas to videotape the performance so that it could be distributed worldwide."

Rachel, Alvin's wife of sixty years, added this, "Alvin always portrays James as unto the Lord. He loves the Word and prayer and spends much of his day in it. I attend many of his dramas and never tire of hearing James' words over and over. He is a hard worker; there's not a lazy bone in his body. He loves his family, and they know they can count on him for spiritual or physical help. He is very funny and one of the most smart and creative people you will ever meet."

Alvin Price is a retired software designer, bass singer for The Masters Men choir of Southeast Christian church, dramatic actor, mentor of men, Bible student and teacher, husband, father of four, grandfather of twelve, great grandfather of fourteen, portrayer of James and follower of Christ. He is not shy with words. Here are a few more of his thoughts.

"James never gets old, and James never quits speaking to me. I have learned so much. If the book of James doesn't hit you where you need to be hit, you are either comatose or lying to yourself. James is a book so full of realistic issues and solutions—even today. As for me, I turn everything over to the Lord many times a day. I try to walk in His peace. I tried the other, and it didn't work.

I love to teach, and I love to study the Bible. I study the Bible every day. God wants us to meet him through his Word, and through His Word, we meet His truth. I am convinced that the Word of God changes people. I ask the Lord that in my appearances, I disappear, and You do this. I don't care if they ever remember my name; may they remember James. I want people to see Christ in me—not Alvin.

James? The drama? It's hard to fail with good material. I'm just trying to let them know what the heart of God sounds like. People do recognize the Word as truth.

Humility? I came loaded with pride, but that all changed. I want to encourage people to put scripture in their heads through memorization. He wants us to know His Word to better know Him. His followers were amazed—we all should be more amazed. The only thing that really matters when we leave this earth is our relationship with Jesus Christ; the rest stays here.

I sure hope this glorifies God, not Alvin. I just want folks to get into the book of James; it will change your life! I stick with the Word because I have a hunger to know God more fully, more accurately, and more deeply. Why? Because I want to be changed into the likeness of his Son. I want the world to be less impressive, less impactful, and less influential to me. I am not a perfect Christian, far from it. In fact, I have spent enough years with myself and applying God's word to know that what I allow Him to do through me is the only redeeming activity in my life. May I learn to give Him everything before my last breath."

Craig

Craig

"Blessed are those who die in the Lord, they will rest from their labor, their deeds will follow them."

Revelation 14:13

Craig was a powerful man. Standing six feet six inches tall, weighing 250 pounds, and in pristine physical condition, he was powerful mentally, physically, emotionally, and spiritually. Craig honed his power as a youth, working on the farms of Western Kentucky and in frequent boyhood skirmishes with his brother, whom he loved so much, Kerry. Though he drove them crazy, he had a powerful love and loyalty for his parents, Bonnie and Larry. He had a powerful love for his wife, Vicki, his son, Adam, and for his close inner circle of friends.

Craig had a powerful love for the gyms, where he spent countless hours, his cars, and later his trucks and RVs. He powerfully loved his church, where he was a leader. More importantly, he had a powerful love for Jesus Christ, integrity, character, leading the way, setting an exemplary example, displaying endless humor and discipline. He powerfully displayed the fruit of the

Spirit—love, joy, peace, patience, kindness, goodness, faithfulness, gentleness, and self-control.

Craig also had a powerful love for athletics. He starred in baseball, basketball, and football—leading his gridiron team to a Kentucky State High School football championship. Later in life, he turned to outdoor adventure sports—kayaking, canoeing, rock climbing, cycling, mountain biking, hiking, camping, and extreme international mountain climbing. Craig was absolutely not to be disturbed (except with food) when the television was tuned to the Kentucky Wildcats or St. Louis Cardinals.

Craig had powerful, consistent, and unwavering belief in all these people and things. As proven by his successful business that still thrives to this day, he was a true entrepreneur who dreamed big, believed big, and succeeded big—despite the doubts of others. He believed. Yes, he believed.

Lest you believe, though, that Craig was a perfect saint, consider this. When in a group, he rarely paid for a restaurant check. He was rousted by countless buffet restaurant owners because of the amount of food he consumed. He never paid for a haircut in his entire life. He had an uncanny ability to get others to do his work for him. He was an average student at best. Legend has it that university officials offered him a diploma if he promised to leave and never return.

He irritated hundreds by out-negotiating them. He had a penchant for getting valuable things for free. As a single man, he rarely, if ever, washed his workout clothes—finding it comical when others left the room because of the stink. When preparing for a major athletic adventure, he ate the exact same thing for dinner every night for weeks—popcorn (no butter) and tuna straight out of the can(s). He exaggerated greatly. For example, he sometimes bragged about his great friend and business partner, Dean, coming into town—on his private jet. (Of course, it never happened—in fact, there was no private jet.) Like his mother, he was sneaky. Like his father, he was frugal (cheap). He was never on time—ever. Craig could be annoying, maddening, and lovable at the same time—much like his chocolate lab, Hooper. The many similarities between dog and owner were uncanny.

It is the tendency of a writer, like me, to overly expound upon their own thoughts, ideas, memories, and opinions. In the story of Craig, I believe it best to hear directly from his beloved inner circle.

One of Craig's fellow adventure enthusiasts, Manley, has vivid memories of his great friend, "Craig was the kind of man who pushed you and inspired you to be a better person every day. But his magic was that he did so while making everyday life incredibly fun. Craig showed me a level of honesty that I didn't know existed. He lived an inspired life of integrity and stayed true to his values, all the while never taking life too seriously. Craig was a devoted friend and deeply committed to supporting your wildest dreams. With Craig in your corner, his love and enthusiasm made you feel like you could take on any mountain in life."

Perhaps Craig's closest friend, Dean, had this to say, "Craig was a mountain of a man with a deep conviction for his faith, family, and friends. He was loyal and always willing to lend a hand, and he inspired people to reciprocate his many traits. He was adventurous and had a passion to constantly challenge himself and others around him. With a wicked sense of humor, Craig could have you laughing at the same time you were in fear for your life. Craig lived his life to the fullest, sharing his many blessings with those closest to him."

Kerry and Craig may have had the tightest brotherly bond most have ever seen. They fought and harassed each other but also defended each other fiercely. Kerry recalls, "Craig was a man of principle. Everyone who knew him knew his word and integrity were unshakable and unmistakable. He was 100 percent loyal to friends and family. He had no tolerance for anyone who spoke badly of those he cared for. Craig was completely loyal to his wife.

He was a devout Christian to the end and inspired many people, especially the young people, with his quiet strength, which was plain to see and very real. He had many friends who loved him because they were drawn to his inner strength and unquestioned integrity. He influenced many, including me, toward Jesus Christ through an unmovable faith and unquestioned character. He always tried to emulate only one person, Jesus Christ. Not a day passes that I don't miss him or his advice, which I sought often. Several of us lost our best friends, including me. I will see him soon."

Another tight brotherly bond existed between Craig and his other brother, Johnny, who he also loved dearly. Johnny laughingly remembers, "Craig could weasel his way out of work better than anyone. He could wait out anyone—for them to do work. When he needed something done, he would call me—or Kerry—or both. He could make money out of nothing, but he was generous. We ate a lot of pizza together. I miss him. I think of him a lot. We respected each other. Just being around him was the best. I spent his last days with him, but we still had fun. I loved Craig."

Craig had a powerful love for his son, Adam. Adam remembers his father, "Craig Sims, my father, was a lot of things to a lot of people. Having only known him for the first twelve years of my life, here are just a few of the things he was to me. He was someone who never met an animal he couldn't nickname, someone who swore he hated cats yet could often be found in his leather recliner with a cat on his belly. He was someone who would ride every roller coaster at Disney World with you, no matter how much it wore him out.

He was someone who considered popcorn as dinner and considered a slice of bread with an egg fried into its middle about the best breakfast you could get anywhere. He was a born outdoorsman who never stopped finding ways to relate to a movie geek son that spent less time out in the fresh air than inside writing letters to Clooney and Schwarzenegger. He was a natural athlete with unlimited patience for the same son being uniquely bad at baseball.

He was someone who was always available for a philosophical discussion—if the discussion could happen in the hot tub. He was the only person who could cheer you up when something catastrophic happened, like losing your fourth-grade spelling bee in the final round. He was one of the funniest people I've ever known, and I only barely got to know him.

Of course, the wife knows the husband best. Vicki offers this, "When I met Craig all those years ago at Murray State, I had no idea where life would take us. When we decided to get married, he promised that our life would never be boring, and his words were so very true. It is said that 'opposites attract,' and mostly for us, that seemed to be the case. He was tall, and I wasn't; he ate a lot, and I didn't. He was a risk-taker; I was not! I was neat and organized; he was not! He preferred extreme physical activity; I was happy to walk.

We were not opposites, however, regarding faith, church, and family. We built a life and a family together around those cornerstones. I didn't know many men who made such an effort; to attend church, be involved there, and live a Christian lifestyle. Craig was certainly one of those. I always loved and appreciated that about him. It was a blessing and a privilege to have been a part of his life. Before his funeral, a comment was made about Craig's age; he was forty-nine. One of his cousins overheard and said, 'Yes, but he packed a lot of living into those forty-nine years!' Yes, he most certainly did."

From childhood to high school, college, the work world, weddings, babies, teenage children, and then funerals, this crew has been through a lot and come out stronger. Craig would be proud. Everyone here has one main thing in common—Craig. They all agree that it's hard to imagine a better man than Craig. It's hard to imagine a more powerful Christian, husband, father, son, brother, or friend. Craig was the best, and he left way too young. But, as Kerry said, "We'll see you soon."

Ed and Thelma Steger

Ed and Thelma

"The mouths of the righteous utter wisdom,
and their tongues speak what is just."

Psalm 37:30

Ed and Thelma Steger, both ninety, have been married sixty-five years. Not every day offers opportunity to have lunch and pick the brains of such a couple, especially since they have been Believers since 1942. They "took me to school" on life, not in the context of preaching but merely in stating simple facts and opinions in plain, ordinary, candid discussion. Ed and Thelma have a few tips on life that are somewhat surprising for folks of their age. They said, "Staying active is important; exercise class twice a week helps. You can't quit because you don't feel good. You must do what you are able to do. If you waited until you felt like it, you wouldn't ever get anything done. Get up early, then stay out of bed. Keep going no matter what. Keep volunteering, no matter what. We remember most everything for some reason. Being older doesn't mean you should stop doing for others."

Modern technology is often overwhelming for senior citizens. Some even stop learning at some point.

Evidently, that is not the case with Ed and Thelma. They commented, "We like e-mail and all that stuff, but truthfully, we don't know how the remote-control works. Most people need to put those cell phones down. Computer games keep your mind sharp, but we don't like to lose. I asked the preacher if he slept with that iPhone. I think he does. Young people ask me why I don't know how to connect new computer things. I ask them if they know how to hook up a horse and buggy."

As veterans of raising children and grandchildren, Ed and Thelma do not mince words. "Who your child dates is a very important issue. A driving force in life is being responsible for those children. Kids in church were never a problem. We each held one, and if one got out of line, I just raised an eyebrow." Sixty-five years of marriage is a remarkable feat. Here are some Steger tips on successful marriage. "Ask yourself before arguing in marriage—is this hill worth dying for? Keep a list of ten non-negotiable issues, then let the rest of everything go. Tactfully challenging each other is an important skill. Always back your spouse publicly after discussing privately."

Marriage sixty-five years ago was quite different than today. Here are some of their fondest memories. "Honeymoon—are you kidding? Being poor eliminates a lot of problems. We did take a vacation one night in St. Louis. My first Christmas gift upon marriage was a hammer, level, square, ladder, and a how-to book. I got the message and got busy. In 1953 we paid twenty-five hundred dollars for a house and property. It worked. We eventually did build bedrooms on to that home—one bedroom at a time, one per year, only when we could afford full payment, and we did as much work ourselves as we possibly could. We did hire a jackleg plumber once but didn't think much of his work—never said much about it."

Some Steger comments have a kernel of truth mixed with wry humor. "Yes, I know that eighty-year-old man, and I've known him since he was two. At our age, if you fall, it's bad. If you fall in the bathroom, it's all over." Ed laughed loudly when he recounted these one-liners, "As a Christian, if a man came to my door to harm my daughter and asked if she was home, I would not lie, but I might kill him. That man once delivered an eleven-minute prayer. I know because I timed him. A friend of ours said he didn't know who an invocation was but said he would pray for them."

Ed and Thelma also threw a few light-hearted punches at this writer; "Dave, your daddy, bless his soul, was the best handyman I have ever seen, but he never thought much of your handyman skills," "Dave, why are you taking so many notes? Can't you remember anything?"

Clearly, the Bible has played a huge role in the lives of Ed and Thelma. Here are a few of their favorites. "We love to laugh, but we also love I Corinthians 14:40, which tells us to do everything in a fitting and orderly way. Our favorite verse is in Hebrews, where we are reminded that Christ endured the Cross with hope. If it's biblical, never let it go. If it's not, let it go. It's best to always do your devotion and prayer in the morning."

Heaven is a subject Ed and Thelma are not afraid of. They responded with more of their light-hearted humor. "We probably won't have any questions for God when we arrive in heaven because He will be so magnificent." Ed said he would like to ask Jesus about the percentage of alcohol that was in that original communion wine. Thelma added, "If you have questions for God now, just let it go." Here are some great basic life lessons from Ed and Thelma, "Don't take yourself too seriously. We like honesty but not negativity. Always go to church. Send hand-written notes and cards to everyone for every occasion. Never miss a good opportunity to keep your mouth shut. Open your heart and speak at the right time. Watch and know every dollar. Love your children and grandchildren. In fact, love everyone—including the ones you don't like. Don't make a big deal out of anything unless it's good. Be on time. Be in the details. Laugh a lot. Go to weddings and funerals; they are important. Keep your marriage vows. Forgive everyone for everything."

I asked Ed if he had any apprehensions about the publication of their viewpoints. He responded, "If it's any good, let's just pass it along and not worry about it." For many reasons, this was one of my all-time favorite lunches, especially since the home-cooked meal was enough itself to write about. Thelma said, "The best way to eat—and the best tasting—is with fresh vegetables, which is why we still work a big garden. Let's go to the garden and pull some turnips!"

Ed and Thelma have since gone to heaven,
but their wisdom lives on.

Toni and Joe Rose

The Roses

> "Flowers appear on the earth; the season of singing has come. The cooing of doves is heard in our land."
>
> Song of Solomon 2:12

Our lawn was adorned with gorgeous rose bushes. I am not a gardener, but fortunately, my neighbor Ralph is. After the first season, Ralph pointed out that I needed to trim the bushes. I was not about to. The bushes were robust and had produced beautiful red roses. Ralph explained the need plus the benefit of even better roses the next year. So, I reluctantly cut back our roses. Six months later, Ralph was right! The transformed roses were amazing. Little did I know, I would soon meet other Roses undergoing major transformation.

Joe and Toni Rose liked to party—every weekend. In fact, they had a lake cabin for that very purpose. On a regular basis, the cabin flowed with beer and fellow partiers. One day, driving to the lake, the Rose family was singing together, happily anticipating another party weekend. Everything changed.

A car slammed into the Rose vehicle. The Roses would

roll several times before finally coming to a stop. Toni and their two young girls, Abbi and Jessi, had injuries, but the major concern was Joe. Toni remembers Joe being unconscious and making ominous gurgling sounds. She feared the worst. Then their car burst into flames. Through perhaps Divine intervention, Toni was able to rescue their daughters and her unconscious husband from the burning vehicle. Toni's first phone call—to her mother—ignited a massive prayer chain back in their hometown. Those prayers evidently sparked more Divine intervention as the family, including Joe, checked out of the hospital just fine after only one night. The transformation of the Roses had begun.

Joe and Toni clearly recall their spiritual lives prior to the accident. They were churchgoers, but by their own admission, they attended primarily out of guilt and were "fans" of Jesus but not "followers." The accident sent Joe and Toni on a search. Toni bawled the entire next church service. The family was filled with gratitude. Things that had been so important to them now seemed insignificant. Their prayer life and focus on Jesus went to a whole new level. Then the questions for the Roses took full bloom. Why did He spare the Roses, and how could they use their gifts and talents to serve Him? What now, Jesus?

On New Year's Eve at the lake cabin, the Rose family decided that instead of making New Year's resolutions, they would ask God what He wanted them to do. Shortly thereafter, Joe went rabbit hunting on their property behind the cabin. Joe and Toni had long discussed a money-making project for the land—condos or perhaps a hotel. But nothing ever materialized. On this day, while walking and hunting that land, Joe said he had an overwhelming sense that God wanted them to build a camp and bring people here—people who didn't have such an opportunity. With a clear vision, Joe went back to the cabin and explained it to Toni. Without batting an eye, Toni agreed. A dream was launched, and plans began to take shape.

The Rose family became consumed with the project as details began to fall into place. They wanted a proper name for their vision but had none until one day, Toni glanced at her phone and saw Isaiah 41:18:

> "I will make rivers flow on barren heights, and springs within the valleys. I will turn the desert into pools of water, and the parched ground into springs. I will put in the desert the cedar and the acacia, the myrtle, and the olive. I will set pines in the wasteland, the fir and the cypress together, so that people may see and

> know, may consider and understand, that the hand of the Lord has done this, that the Holy One of Israel has created it."

Since their lake cabin was located on the Barren River, the name became obvious—Barren Heights.

The final piece of the early puzzle was who to invite. The answer came quickly and easily to the Roses. Instead of throwing parties for friends, beer, and craziness, Joe and Toni began honoring families with special needs children. Most of their guest families cannot afford a vacation. They stay in first-class facilities with top-notch food. They are loved by the Roses and their volunteers. They enjoy recreation and worship. The parents are afforded a rare respite from 24/7 care of their children. In addition to their primary mission, Barren Heights provides weekends for men and women ministries as well as marriage mentoring. Weekends, year-round, are very special at Barren Heights. The Roses have made wise use of their property behind their cabin, and God has done great things with His promise from Isaiah.

Today, after eighteen years, Barren Heights has thrived amidst hard work, selfless volunteers, blessings, and obvious miracles. Founders Joe and Toni, while still active in the ministry, have stepped back from their leadership roles to infuse new energy from the next generation. Their daughter, Abbi, Executive Director, now superbly leads the two Barren Heights sites and all operations—which have been financially sound from day one.

Joe and Toni reflect on their nearly two-decade adventure. "We are so proud of the ministry and of Abbi's leadership. But it's never really been about us. It's about the families we serve and God, who put us in a place to have this opportunity. It's been a faith journey He has led us on. We felt ill-equipped at times, but we kept going knowing that God would keep sending just the right help at just the right time plus, we know Barren Heights has always been bathed in prayer. We've tried to do things with excellence, but it's really much bigger than us."

Transformed Roses are indeed amazing.

Marquita, Isaiah, Tyrell, & Elijah
The Grant Family

Transformed in His Image

> "Do not conform to the pattern of this world but be transformed by the renewing of your mind. then you will be able to test and approve what God's will is—his good, pleasing, and perfect will."
>
> Romans 12:2

Tyrell Grant was only nine years old when his father died. Tyrell, the youngest of nineteen children, had also lost two sisters to death. He said, over time, those losses left him angry with God. Tyrell said he often wondered, "Where is God?" At the age of twenty-two, Tyrell, without a father figure, found himself with little direction in life. He enjoyed drinking and was a regular in St. Louis nightclubs. He described himself as stubborn and strong-willed. He was, in his words, living for himself and searching for meaning in his life.

But everything changed. Tyrell, now twenty-seven, is a successful minister of the gospel of Jesus Christ. How does such a radical transformation occur in less than five years? Tyrell said it all began upon moving to Paducah, KY, in 2011 when his wife, Marquita, insisted he attend church. He had little interest. Tyrell said, "To get Marquita off my back, I started going to church." The transformation had begun. Tyrell was soon surrounded by another family—Marquita's church family, the Broadway Church of Christ in Paducah. Tyrell said, "You can't find a better bunch of people. They love me, and they have flooded me with encouragement. They go above and beyond. I love them all."

Tyrell also found himself captivated by the sermons of Broadway Teaching Minister Dr. Dan Owen. Tyrell said, "Dan spoke the Word, and the Word spoke to me." Tyrell began looking forward to Sunday mornings in church. The next link in Tyrell's transformational chain was forged when Owen somewhat abruptly asked him if he wanted to study the Bible. Tyrell surprised even himself with his quick and positive response. Tyrell and Dan did indeed study—for many, many hours. Their studies fostered a strong friendship that continues to this day. Dan said he even considers Tyrell his "adopted son." Tyrell had this to say about Dan, "He's a really great guy. He loves God, and he loves people. He has helped me so much. He's doing the work of the Lord." A few months after they met, Dan baptized Tyrell into Christ.

Another man entering Tyrell's life was Mike Moore. Tyrell noted, "Mike has played a major role in my spiritual development." Mike, a Paducah attorney and church elder, said, "Tyrell is a great, great husband and father. He is a very smart man and a very motivated student. He so totally believes in the Gospel, and he'll do whatever it takes to convey it. He is a great leader in the making, and I think God has big plans for him." Major changes in the life of Tyrell would continue. His priorities were turned upside down. He had transformed from a seeker of pleasure to a sacrificial servant. Tyrell found that his thirst for the Word of God seemed unquenchable. He studied his Bible constantly. He prayed on a regular basis. He credits Dan and Mike for instilling that passion, but Tyrell also said he knows that it was God who created that zeal.

The more Tyrell studied, the more captivated he became with one thought. How could he repay God for the incredible gift he had been given? Ultimately, Tyrell knew that he wanted to preach like he had been preached to. He wanted to teach like he had been taught. He wanted to disciple like those who had led him. He might be new in his faith, but he knew how he could give back what had been given him. He knew what he wanted to do. He had a plan, and he wasted little time. At Dan's leadership, Tyrell began shadowing Dan in every aspect of ministry. Tyrell said his decision to become a preacher of the Gospel was a natural way for him to express his new focus in life.

"Having something from God to say to others is an awesome feeling because it's all about Him, not me. I like to make very much of Him and very little of me. I was very nervous before my first sermon, but when I finished, I was on cloud nine." Evidently, he is not the only one on cloud nine. Broadway enthusiastically embraced the young minister. One long-time member commented, "When Tyrell spoke, I felt God was speaking directly to me. He speaks from the heart. He has a humble spirit and a natural gift for teaching." Tyrell began as an intern and assistant minister at Broadway and has preached over twenty sermons at various churches during his young ministerial career. And Tyrell has the strong endorsement of his mentor. Dan said, "For many, interest in being a minister is often fleeting, but it didn't take long to know that Tyrell was very serious about every aspect of ministry. He is sincere and highly motivated. He has great communication skills and has all types of talent. He is a gifted evangelist. God is really working in his life."

Preaching is but one of Tyrell's new passions. He said he's been given a natural love of the scriptures and wants to share that knowledge one on one. He has a strong desire to disciple others as he was himself. "Teaching souls about Jesus is all that's important," he said. In addition to teaching congregations, classes and individuals, Tyrell also focuses on his own ongoing education. He attended Bear Valley Bible Institute, where he continued to accelerate his learning. Tyrell said, "I want to hear and learn, but most importantly, I want to do it."

Tyrell and Marquita also have a love for children as they own a successful business, a children's daycare facility in Paducah, The Early Learning Academy. A primary passion of the Grants is their own family. They are the proud parents of a young son, Elijah, who was born prematurely. In that hour of concern, who was at the hospital to offer prayer and support? Members of the Broadway Church of Christ showed up in a big way again. Tyrell said, "Our church family was there when we needed them most. Now we try to do the same and be there for others." And by the way, Elijah is doing fine. Tyrell's humility and sense of humor are often on display, as was evidenced by his comment, "What I've done is no big deal. I just started showing up at Broadway, got baptized, and stayed. No one ran me off."

But Tyrell's sincerity is far beyond superficial. When asked to name a biblical hero, he responded, "Well, obviously Jesus Christ. I could never say enough. He was courageous, loving, caring, and a leader who wasn't afraid to shake things up. He was the greatest leader to ever live. We worship an amazing and mighty God." As for his favorite Bible verse, Tyrell mentions Philippians 4:8:

> "Finally, brothers, whatever is true, whatever is noble, whatever is right, whatever is pure, whatever is lovely, whatever is admirable, if anything is excellent or praiseworthy, think about such things."

He adds, "This is the best way I know of to stay positive." When asked about his preaching so soon in his relatively new relationship with Christ, Tyrell refers to another of his biblical heroes Paul, the author of another of his favorite verses. "After his conversion to Christ, Paul immediately went and began to preach the Word." I'm no Paul, but that's what I want to do—immediately go and preach the Word. When my eyes were opened (like Paul's), I wanted to study as hard as I could and do as much as I could. I can't earn anything, but I do want to give back to Him what He gave to me. As for being young, maybe twenty years from now, I'll have a fraction of Dan's knowledge, but I won't wait till then. I say just go do it now."

Tyrell, who appears far beyond his years in terms of wisdom and insight, said he learned wise risk-taking from Marquita. "She took a risk with me. I want that to pay off for all of us. Marquita has taught me a lot. She is patient, willing to help, good-hearted, kind, funny, and smart. She is unafraid to fail. Now, neither am I. Twenty years from now, I want it to be known that I preach Christ—even if it upsets some people. I'll follow Christ. Everything else will fall into place."

Marquita, to no surprise, has high praise for her husband. "Tyrell is an awesome husband and father. He is trustworthy. From where he was to where he is today is awesome. His change happened quicker than I could ever imagine, but that's the kind of guy he is. Whatever he puts his mind to, he dives in headfirst and does it to the best of his ability." Apparently, the seeds planted by Marquita, Dan, Mike, and others are bearing much fruit in the life of Tyrell. A once angry young man has found peace. Through Marquita, he has found direction. Through the Broadway Church of Christ, he found a platform for his new passions. Through Christ, he has found a Lord and Savior. Tyrell Grant is a transformed man on a mission—a mission for Christ.

Earl Gidcumb

Taps

> "Know that the Lord has set apart his faithful servant for himself; the Lord hears when I call to him."
>
> Psalm 4:3

Earl Gidcumb, eighty-eight, has played "Taps" at veteran gravesite services for over seventy-five years. Though he resides in the tiny town of Wickliffe, Kentucky, he has far-reaching notoriety. Earl, himself a decorated World War II veteran, is a devoted grandfather, father, husband, and friend. He is a talented musician and still plays golf. Most importantly to him, he is a passionate believer and follower of Jesus Christ. This extraordinary life of service began when Earl's grandparents gave him a trumpet in 1936 at the age of ten.

"God gave me a gift, and He has been by my side ever since," he said. "He blessed me with a talent, and I thank Him for that every day." Earl became a professional trumpet player in 1952, playing various locales for more than thirty years. Along the way, he met legendary trumpet players such as Louis Armstrong, Al Hirt, and Dave Brubeck. Though Earl has performed in many churches in his career, his first religious rendition began on a humorous note. He declined an invitation to play at a local church because he had played in a nightclub the previous night. The minister reminded him that some of his parishioners had likely been in his audience the night before. Earl laughed and accepted.

His nightclub performances are long in the past, but he plays in churches to this day. Perhaps Earl's most notable tune is his rendition of "Taps" as a final salute to veterans. If you have ever heard a lone trumpeter playing "Taps" at a funeral, it may have been Earl. He began this service, which has always been free, in 1940. He has played "Taps" at hundreds of funeral services, though he can't remember the exact number. "Most eighty-eight-year-old people lose their teeth. I believe my lip may be wearing out," he said. "My performing days may be nearing an end, but I'll play as long as the good Lord wants me to." With so few World War II veterans still living, Earl does have a plan for who will play "Taps" at his funeral. "I'm not sure there will be anyone left by then, so I recorded my own rendition of 'Taps' that can be played at my burial," he said.

Earl's decorated military career was highlighted by his service during World War II on the USS Indianapolis, a heavy cruiser in the U.S. Navy's Fifth Fleet. Earl joined the crew of the Indianapolis in 1944 while stationed in Pearl Harbor, and he received five battle stars in his ten months aboard the ship. A few months after Earl was transferred off the Indianapolis, it was sunk by a Japanese submarine. Of the 1,196 men aboard, only 317 survived. Hundreds of men were cast into the Pacific Ocean, and by the time rescue arrived four days later, many had perished from drowning, hypothermia, or shark attack, leading to the greatest loss of life at sea in U.S. Naval history.

Earl said, "The second torpedo of the two that struck the Indianapolis hit the part of the ship where I slept each night. I would not have survived, and I would not be here today if I had not been transferred," Earl said. "For some reason, God took me off that ship. He had a plan." Earl later served aboard the USS Bottineau, a troop carrier. "I saw men put in LCVP vessels (landing crafts) and sent to do battle on the beach to take the island back from the Japanese. I saw some of the same men brought back in body bags," said Earl in a recent tribute read on the floor of the U.S. Senate.

"I saw 450 Japanese planes shot down in the Battle of the Philippine Sea, all in one day. I saw a Japanese Zero so close that I could see the orange Japanese flag on the side of the plane. I saw body parts of Japanese soldiers scattered everywhere when I went over the Island of Tarawa. We lost 8,000 Marines of our own. This was my first battle." Earl is extremely proud to be a veteran. He still attends reunions for the Indy survivors, of which only eighty-four remain.

He still plays his trumpet every day, but that is not the major focus of his life. "I became a Christian in 1963 and have been an imperfect but saved Christian all along," he said. "He has carried me through many good times and many bad times. I always knew He was there. Jesus means everything to me. Even in illness, God has been there. My first wife became seriously ill. I nursed her many months until her death," he said. "Now, my second wife has health problems. I hope the Lord will take care of me so that I can take care of her. God has carried us through all of this, and I thank Him every day."

Earl Gidcumb left to be with his Lord in 2017.
A recording of his rendition of Taps
was played at his burial.

Bill Keightley

Mr. Wildcat

> "Whatever you do, work at it with all your heart, as working for the Lord, not for human masters."
>
> Colossians 3:23

Bill Keightley was a simple, hard-working farm boy who delivered mail for forty years. But during that career, Keightley worked a second job that made him a Kentucky legend. When Keightley died in April 2008, his state-like funeral was held in front of thousands at Rupp Arena in Lexington, KY. Hall of Fame coaches, famous athletes, political dignitaries, postal employees, and everyday folks of Kentucky all came to pay their respects. The event was a testimony to the tremendous influence he had on people of all ages during his decades of service to the Postal Service and the University of Kentucky basketball program. Perhaps no equipment manager in the history of sports has received such acclaim.

His daughter, Karen Keightley Marlowe, is now in her twenty-fifth year as an employee in the UK. Fittingly, she is the first voice that callers hear when they phone the UK Athletic Department. Marlowe provided the information for this story of faith, love, and UK basketball. Marlowe said the roots of the Keightley family are grounded deep in a strong faith in Jesus Christ. Keightley and his wife Hazel, ninety-three, had long ago set their sights on living a Christian life. "My mother is a wonderful, wonderful lady who always lived a good Christian life," Marlowe said. "She and Daddy had a great marriage, and I could not have asked for better parents."

The family rarely missed church. "I was raised by Christian parents in a Christian household," Marlowe said. "There was never any question. Those values guide everything I do and every decision I make." At the age of thirteen, while in church, Marlowe said she felt someone squeeze her shoulder, but no one was behind her. "I was touched, and I knew immediately it was Jesus. I accepted the Lord and have been a Christian ever since." Keightley loved being a letter carrier, according to Marlowe. As he did as an early-rising farm boy, Keightley started his mail days well before dawn. He typically rose at 4 a.m., delivered mail, and then headed to the UK for another full day's work. After a UK road trip, he would often get no sleep for more than twenty-four hours. In the early days of his UK role, Keightley washed and folded towels and uniforms. It was that type of humble work, like delivering mail, that Keightley never shied away from.

In his latter days at UK, Keightley, while maintaining his equipment manager role, served as a highly regarded informal mentor and counselor to both players and coaches. "Daddy helped others because that's the kind of person he was," Marlowe said. "He was a natural mentor who loved people. He was a kind, empathetic person who enjoyed giving of himself." Keightley became the "go-to-guy" for players who were having trouble adjusting to academics, being away from home, their coaches, or the demands of performing in a high-profile basketball program. Usually, the informal discussions took place in the equipment room. Players evidently knew where to go when things went wrong. "He often was the father figure to athletes who never had a father," Marlowe said. "He was just so positive, and he could help players see the light at the end of the tunnel. What happened outside the games was where Daddy's value lay. Because of Daddy and so many others, boys leave the UK with better character, and we're proud of that."

Coaches also held Keightley in high regard. Coach Joe B. Hall promoted Keightley to full-time equipment manager. Coach Rick Pitino gave Keightley the first seat on the bench during UK games. Though it was a seat of honor,

Keightley couldn't imagine why he was chosen. He said, "Why in the world do they want me here?" He was told that his first job was to "reel in Rick and avoid technical fouls when things got heated." When Keightley made his first in-game attempt at peacemaking, Pitino turned on him and said, "Sit down and shut up." Keightley recalled, "I'm obviously not qualified for this bench job!"

Pitino and Keightley both referred to each other as the most unique man they had ever met. "A man from New York City and a country boy from Lawrenceburg, KY, should have nothing in common but they did, specifically work ethic and what they believed about the UK program," Marlowe said. "They had more similarities than differences, and they had a special bond." Keightley may have learned to stay seated on the UK bench, but his passion for the UK, from the seat of honor, was always evident—to the home crowd and the television audience.

His huge smile and his grimaces became legendary. He was lovingly referred to as "Mr. Bill," "Mr. Wildcat," and "Big Smooth." He made friends from Dick Vitale to "Joe from Paducah." Keightley's keen sense of humor and trademark laugh often found their way to center stage. When Pitino accepted the head coaching job at arch-rival University of Louisville, Keightley received one of the first phone calls from Pitino. Keightley reportedly said, "Rick, have you lost your mind?" Marlowe has her own take on UK coaches, "We love Joe B. He is an awesome gentleman. Rick is a super person, and he has been incredible to us. He is a very kind man. He once bought Daddy a new truck—because he loved him and because Daddy's truck was about to fall apart! We still love Tubby (Smith). His kindness and quality of character make him one of the finest humans I have ever met. Coach Gillispie depended heavily on Daddy."

Keightley was part of three UK NCAA Championships. He is a member of the Kentucky Athletic Hall of Fame. His retired jersey (No. 48—for forty-eight years of service) now hangs in the rafters of Rupp Arena. The Keightleys have been associated with UK athletics since the days of legendary UK basketball coach Adolph Rupp. They feel blessed to be part of the UK family. Yet, basketball does not define their lives. Love and service do. Marlowe said it all began with church and Jesus Christ. "Daddy didn't preach; he would just love, give and serve," Marlowe said. "He had the Christian spirit, and he shared it with others. He had humility. He never understood why he was so popular. He was just a regular guy, and his popularity happened because he was just himself.

If he were here, he would say, 'Work hard, try your best, stay positive, do the right thing, always tell the truth.' He always said that loving each other is so important." Evidently, Keightley's roots in Jesus Christ grew into something extraordinarily special as he evolved into an inspiration to thousands. He never sought honor, but it sure found him. Sometimes the most important guy is in the background washing towels.

Mr. Wildcat went to heaven in 2008.
His legacy of love, humility, and service is carried on
by Hazel, Karen, and hundreds of others.

Harold Kratch

Soldier Follows Christ

"Now all has been heard; here is the conclusion of the matter: Fear God and keep his commandments, for this is the duty of all mankind."

Ecclesiastes 12:13

He seemed like an ordinary elderly man. In fact, as I taught a Bible study class, Harold Kratch seemed to be annoying and time-consuming because, after class, he inundated me each week with new teaching material. Harold turned out to be anything but a time-consuming, ordinary, elderly man. Once after class, in an impulsive effort to accelerate his usual diatribe, I invited him to breakfast to discuss all his thoughts. Thus, in the fall of 2002, an extraordinary friendship began. Over bacon and eggs, Harold, age eighty-four at the time, quickly established himself as an individual with a vast array of experiences, a sharp memory, a quick wit, and an excellent grasp of scripture. From that day forward, we began meeting on a regular basis.

I learned a lot from Harold. I used much of his material in my teaching. I twice gave Harold the microphone, and he once fascinated a crowd of more than 200 with his knowledge of the significance and details of the lineage of Abraham. On another, he held the attention of large crowds of students with his stories as a veteran of World War II and the Korean War.

As part of the Greatest Generation, Army Lt. Harold Kratch once led a unit of men in France who were caught unprepared for an enemy air attack. With little way to protect his men, Harold impulsively knelt on the battlefield and prayed. There were no injuries in the bombing. In fact, over the next 18 months, Harold's unit fought through Europe, North Africa, and Italy without experiencing a single significant injury. On the last night of his unit's assignment together in an olive grove in Italy, one of his men told Harold that they had confidence in his leadership because of his boldness in the battlefield prayer. Harold credited the prayer to a sudden memory from his elementary school days, a portrait of George Washington kneeling in prayer on the battlefield. Harold later wrote a book, One Soldier's Memories.

In what would turn out to be our final breakfast, I explained to Harold some adversities I was enduring. When I asked for his advice, he paused and then said, "I can only think of one thing to say—the last verse of Ecclesiastes, "Here is the conclusion of the matter, fear God and keep

His commandments for this is the whole duty of man."

A few weeks after that breakfast, Harold's wife, Marge, called to let me know of his death. After a brief conversation, I asked her how she knew to call me since we had never met. She said, "Harold kept a shortlist in his wallet—people to inform upon his death. He said these were the only ones who listened to him when he was an old man." I learned many lessons from Harold, but mostly, I learned to listen, not speak. I learned to never dismiss elderly people. They should be honored and respected. Oftentimes, they are young treasures trapped in an older body.

I would never attempt to summarize the life of a ninety-four-year-old man whom I only knew for ten years, but I do know that Harold was a fine soldier, engineer, author, biblical scholar, husband, father, grandfather, and follower of Christ. I am grateful to have had him as a friend and mentor. I believe I'll pay closer attention to "ordinary" elderly people. They probably aren't so ordinary after all. I look forward to breakfast with Harold in heaven.

Lt. Harold Kratch was promoted to heaven in 2012.

Alphonso Young

Shoeshine, Anyone?

> "Trust in the Lord with all your heart and lean not on your own understanding; in all your ways submit to him, and he will make your paths straight."
>
> Proverbs 3:5-6

The Louisville KY International Airport is home to a ministry cleverly disguised as a shoeshine stand. Alphonso Young has owned and operated his shoe service for more than twenty-seven years in this location and several others. During my recent visit, he rarely mentioned the word "shoe." "My ministry here is to talk to people who don't know Christ, to help them get to know Christ and share with them what the Lord has done for me and what the Lord can do for them," Alphonso said. Evidently, shoes are Alphonso's secondary profession.

"I'm here to take care of God's business," he said. "He's the one who put me here, and He is the one who has guided me all these years. He's the one I look to for all the help I need. He teaches me and tells me what to do and when to do it. I could do this differently, but His way is the best way. By doing that, I know I'm going to make it." Travelers stopping by one of Alphonso's stands likely get a little more than they expected. For five dollars, they receive a shoeshine but also a word of encouragement. "The Lord has sent me here to encourage through a word from Him," he said. "I want them to see the face of Christ in me. That's what I'm here for."

Alphonso's soft-spoken but enthusiastic Gospel message is not limited to travelers. Many shiners Alphonso has hired are those who need encouragement in life. "We have helped a lot of people and taught them how to conduct themselves in business through the approach of Christ," he said. "In turn, they become ministers to their customers. Many of my employees have even gone on to become full-time ministers." Alphonso has shined the shoes of mayors, congressmen, and well-known celebrities, but evidently, no one is immune to his infectious message.

"Yes, I have served some famous people, but mostly I shine the shoes of ordinary people," he said. "No matter who, I have the opportunity to mention God." Though some may look down on shoeshine men, Alphonso considers shining shoes an honor. "Jesus set the example for me by humbling Himself and washing the disciples' feet," he said. Alphonso and his shoeshine gear have traveled all over the world. "The Lord has opened doors for me I would never have believed," he said.

I barely got in a word in this interview, and that's probably best. Alphonso's words are rapid, and they strike the heart. He continued, "Why did he take a little fellow from Louisville and send him around the world shining shoes? I believe it was to encourage people through His Word. Every time I have traveled, I've had the opportunity to tell people about the Lord. I've been following Christ for thirty years. There is no other way to go but to Him, by Him, and through Him. Nothing compares to what God can do. He owns the world and everything in it. Without Him, we can do nothing. He is the great I Am. Nothing else can compare to Jesus Christ, my Lord and Savior. Without Him, nothing can be done. With Him, nothing is impossible. I thank Him for the opportunity to be a vessel in this ministry."

As for retirement and his future, Alphonso has some very definite plans: "I'll do this until He tells me to change, then I'll do what He tells me to do. Until that time, I'll keep on doing it His way. I believe in Proverbs 3:5–6:

> 'Trust in the Lord with all your heart. Lean not on your own understanding. In all your ways acknowledge Him, and He will make your paths straight.' I stand on that scripture. I am sold out to Him.'"

Mitch Barnhart

Ministry Over Athletics

"Therefore, everyone who hears these words of mine and puts them into practice is like a wise man who built his house on the rock."

Matthew 7:24

When asked about the role of faith in his professional life, University of Kentucky Director of Athletics Mitch Barnhart said he wants to be known as a proud follower of Jesus Christ. "I hope that faith plays a major role in my life, not just in my job," he said. "If I get that right, it permeates everything I do in my life. I may have failed miserably at times, but that relationship with Jesus Christ gives me great peace and allows me to make decisions as to what Jesus wants me to do as opposed to what Mitch wants to do." Mitch has served as the UK's director of athletics since 2002, and while the UK is well known for national prominence in basketball, Mitch seems to spend as much time promoting all twenty-two UK sports teams and the importance of faith in those programs. For example, Mitch said the UK, in the past, has taken athletes to serve children in Ethiopia.

Though he takes no personal credit, Mitch also points

to individual success, like the young man who visited his office recently to announce he had accepted Jesus Christ. Mitch noted, "He wasn't one that I expected that of. I get as excited about these things as I do about some of the teams we have beaten. Hopefully, we have moved the needle in terms of helping these athletes focus on what is truly important." Noticeably missing from Mitch's fingers and office are the five national championship rings from his tenure at the UK. (The rifle team has won three, the men's basketball team has won one, as has the women's volleyball team.)

He is quick to point to a higher cause. "I have the rings at home in a drawer," he said. "They are nice and are great for memories, but I sure hope they don't define me. I'd much rather be defined by more important things. I hope the seeds we plant here in the UK bear great fruit whether we see it or not. That's how I want our program to be defined." As for the roots of his own faith journey, when Mitch was 11, his father announced he had accepted Jesus Christ. Eight months later, at the age of thirty-six, his father died of cancer. "So, my father did not get to be a mentor for very long, but he taught me great lessons and had a great impact on my life. Obviously, I give my mom great credit for training me as well," he said.

For other mentors, Mitch credits former coach and sports administrator Doug Dickey and Mike Hamilton, former AD at the University of Tennessee. "Mitch hired me, and I have known him for over twenty years," Hamilton said. "I appreciate him very much as a person. In the role of AD, you will face hard times, criticism, and crisis. Mitch has always been there with prayer or an appropriate Bible verse. We have connected in our faith far beyond professionalism and have grown closer to Christ through our successes as well as our brokenness. Mitch had this to say of his spiritual colleagues, "From time to time, I seek counsel from men like these to make sure I'm doing what Christ wants me to do and to hold me accountable to that. Jesus didn't talk about loving or forgiving or giving—he loved, forgave, and gave. I want to be relational with those people who do it, not just talk about it, men like Jay Jacobs (former AD at Auburn University). I admire men who have been through the battles and continue to walk their talk, men who are willing to get their hands dirty, men who love, forgive, and give.

So, how would Mitch like to be remembered in the UK? "How awful would it be if I were defined merely by national championships," he said. "What keeps me grounded is the cross I wear around my neck. It reminds me every moment of who I want to be. "I'm far from perfect, but in some way, when people look at what I have done, they will say there is something different about the way Mitch does business. They may not like it or agree with it, but when they look deeper, they will find that I have an ongoing working relationship with Jesus Christ and move people to be doers and not just talk about it. I hope when people look at what we are doing in Kentucky, they will notice these things. Oh, and by the way, we've done a few things athletically at the UK that have turned out okay."

Because he has placed his focus on serving God and living for Him, Mitch said that he shies away from focusing on his personal accomplishments, which is difficult in a position that largely is judged by wins and losses and revenue generated for one of the nation's most high-profile athletic departments. "We all want to be successful, but I don't think much about awards or my legacy," Mitch said. "I would like people to know that I have been married to the same wonderful gal for thirty-nine years, I have three beautiful kids, four adorable grandchildren, two wonderful sons-in-law, an awesome daughter-in-law, and I am a proud follower of Jesus Christ."

Alcohol Loses

"He must become greater; I must become less."

John 3:30

Hense Bennett was a drunk, but a simple invitation to a Bible study set him on a path toward transformation. Hense said he got drunk for the first time at age eleven and eventually drank his way through three universities. "Some people drink two beers at a party; I drank fifteen," he said. Despite his binge drinking, he was a collegiate athlete and earned an MBA from the University of Kentucky. Upon graduation, Hense moved to Louisville, married in 1990, started a family, and began a stellar business career.

The drinking followed him. "I began drinking early in the morning and throughout the day," he said. "I kept bottles of liquor under the seat of my car. I would slip away from work to sneak a glassful. I drank on and off every day and into the evening. I was a functioning alcoholic, but it got to the point I couldn't function without alcohol. I knew I had to stop, but I had no answers." In 2006, friend Dave Shutt, a Louisville dentist, invited Hense to attend a weekly men's Bible study. He accepted the invite and often attended the 6:30 a.m. meeting under the influence of alcohol. "I accepted Jesus in 2006, but I did not stop drinking," Hense said. Though his spiritual journey was beginning, things got worse for Hense.

In 2008, he was fired from his job, and he spent days at home drinking alone. "One night, I looked up at the sky and began sobbing," he said. "I told God He had to help me. I knew I was in trouble." Shortly thereafter, Hense told friends and family that he needed help with his alcohol addiction. "That confession brought a great sense of peace," he said. "They knew I was drinking too much, but no one had a clue how much." Five days later, Hense enrolled in a rehabilitation center in Alabama. "For the first time in my life, I got really, really honest," he said. "I didn't need to lie and cover up anymore. My honesty and transparency brought tremendous peace. The Alcoholics Anonymous twelve-step program worked for me because I took it very seriously and followed each step precisely. The guys from my Bible study supported me throughout. They sent me letters and a Bible. They prayed for me. I am so grateful. I am one of the few who succeed in their first rehab experience. I am now ten years sober."

Despite success in rehab, Hense's return to Louisville was difficult. His marriage, family, finances, and professional career were in shambles. In 2010, his wife asked for a divorce. He remembers leaving home with his car, some clothes, and seventy-three dollars. "I lost most everything, but I did not take a drink and still haven't," he said. "I credit God, the men's Bible study, and Southeast Christian Church, where I had joined in 2009. No one there told me what I did was okay, but there was no condemnation or fierce judgment. I was always welcomed and encouraged. The Southeast sermons spoke to my heart. I was hearing the truth, in love, and the Gospel for the first time in my life. It made a huge difference."

Hense continues to attend the weekly men's Bible study, and he said the men in the group strengthen him, encourage him, and hold him accountable. "Hense is true to his faith," said Shutt. "He stays in the Word and prayer. I'm proud of him. He has struggles, but he keeps Christ the main thing in his life." Hense attends and now leads twelve-step recovery programs; he mentors men with addiction issues and recently traveled to Scotland on a mission trip to help addicts in Scottish slums.

"Life is tough. Though I am still sober, I am challenged professionally and financially, and I have a host of health issues," he said. "But I have incredible blessings. God has always provided. I have a strong relationship with

God—a relationship with real meaning." "I have become really good friends with Hense," said Pastor Greg Allen. "I deeply appreciate his transparency about his journey. He has been humbled, but I greatly respect his faithfulness. I also appreciate his heart to help other alcoholics and in leading them to Christ."

One of Hense's favorite verses is John 3:30, which says, "'He must become greater, I must become less." "Jesus is the only answer," he said. "I just need to get out of the way because it's not about me. I want to serve because look at how He served me on the cross. I have incredible gratitude. I have deep sorrow and regret for the people I hurt and the pain I caused, but I am grateful my journey turned me to God. Otherwise, I wouldn't have Him in my life. I do, at times, feel like I'm hanging on by a thread, but really, I'm right in the palm of His hand."

Hense recently celebrated thirteen years of sobriety.

Military Ministry

> "He said to them, "Go into all the world and preach the gospel to all creation."
>
> Matthew 16:15

U.S. Marine Corps Captain Jacob Sims has successfully participated in military missions in nine countries. But another of Jacob's missions is sharing the message of Jesus Christ. While stationed overseas, he has led small group Bible studies patterned from his experiences at Southeast Christian Church in Louisville, where he remains an online, long-distance member. "I joined the military because of patriotism and a deep desire to serve and give back to what was given to me," Jacob said. "We live in the greatest country in the history of the world. I did nothing to earn that. I was just lucky to be born in the USA. I am eternally blessed by those before me who were willing to sacrifice. That's humbling. I have a responsibility to answer the call of duty."

Jacob has led, at times, up to 300 soldiers into military operations. "The Bible offers the best guidance for leadership style—it teaches good judgment, making good decisions, and taking personal responsibility," he added. "Good leadership comes naturally to those of faith. A leader must be genuine and caring as well as stern and supportive at the same time." Jacob said he gains great fulfillment in seeing his junior officers develop and succeed with that leadership style. "You try to mentor and lead. You hope your investment pays off," he said. "It's a proud moment when you see them have major success. I pray for them. To see their faith grow is extremely gratifying. I lead, but it's not me. It's God."

Nick Williams, now a federal investigator in Texas, served alongside Jacob in the Marines. "There are some outstanding Christian men and women in the military, but mostly it's a godless world," Williams said. "I could tell immediately that Jacob was a Godly man who was very devoted to family. He was the first to start a Bible study for many troops, whether they were Christian or not. He is very passionate about spreading the Word and building relationships. He was the first true Christian friend I had in the military. He helped me build my faith. Jacob is kind and compassionate to others. He is a great leader. He has greatly impacted, spiritually, the men and women who have served under him."

Jacob and his wife, Kara, experienced the power of Christian community while part of a small church group.

"We went through a tough time with the birth of our first child," Kara said. "Our small group surrounded us with love (and food!) for weeks on end. Small groups taught us to love and set the foundation for us. We want to follow that example. Pastor Max Semenick led the first small group the Sims attended and officiated their wedding. "I knew right from the beginning that Jacob was a leader," Max said. "Jacob and Kara have a deep sense of honor and tradition. They are some of my favorite folks. I see them as a couple who deeply love each other, family, and Jesus."

Jacob describes his dual missions as very simple. "We are to love God with all our heart, love your neighbor as yourself and go out and make disciples," he said. "I try to be a servant leader the best I can. I'm not perfect, but I try to do the right things even when no one is watching. And I know that as a leader, people are watching all the time. I began to really grow my own personal faith at Southeast. That time was a great beginning for Kara and me."

The Sims family, which includes three small children, relocated to Japan, which brought a new set of challenges. "Our furniture and belongings were delayed, and we were driving on the left side of the road dealing with a language we didn't know," Kara said. "We knew no one, and we were living in Japan where only 2% of the population is

Christian. We were stressed and worried that we would not have a Christian community to connect with." But a small Christian group, once again, came to the rescue. "I'm so happy we found each other. They welcomed us with open arms," Kara said. "Military families have no natural families here, so we have to be Jesus for each other. Everyone just walks beside each other. Jacob often leads the group meetings. It's been a huge challenge here, but we are doing fine with the help of our small group. Our small group mirrors Jesus in person, and that's important because Jesus is the one and only constant you can count on."

"We learned that things are challenging and complex here in Japan, but it is not the big picture; Jesus is," Jacob added. "After seeing warfare and evil up close, things don't bother me as much. We have better perspective, and we remember what is truly important. What the Gospel says is hard but simple. Love God, love people, and disciple. We've just got to stay focused on the main thing."

The Sims continue their adventures—
now stationed in Hawaii.

Wingmen

> "As iron sharpens iron, so one person sharpens another."
>
> Proverbs 27:17

The United States Air Force defines "wingman" as a pilot who supports another pilot in a potentially dangerous flying environment. Wingman, as displayed in the motion picture "Top Gun," was originally a term referring to the plane flying beside and slightly behind the lead plane in an aircraft formation. According to Air Force sources, the wingman's role is to add an element of mutual support. The presence of a wingman makes the flight both offensively and defensively more capable of increasing situational awareness.

The wingman's mere presence minimizes attack by the enemy and increases the ability to employ more dynamic tactics. The wingman protects the lead pilot by watching his back. The wingman's primary responsibilities are remaining close to the leader and warning the leader of any immediate threats. Air Force Lt. Col. Robert Smith describes the responsibilities as mutually exclusive, and "wingmen are expected to remain with the leader." The Air Force clearly understands the critical role of the wingman.

Retired Air Force Col. Don Waddell flew 151 combat missions as a fighter pilot. He said, "How important is a wingman? How important is your partner in doubles tennis? A wingman is another set of eyes and ears (and often another brain), who provides mutual support." The relationship between pilot and wingman was demonstrated in a negative way on January 19, 1982, when the lead pilot of the Thunderbirds, the Air Force aerial demonstration team, experienced a flight control malfunction while practicing aerobatics.

The four-ship flight was coming out of a loop heading straight down when Lt. Col. Norm Lowery's aircraft malfunctioned. Before he could analyze the situation and tell three wingmen to abort the maneuver, all four aircraft crashed into the Nevada desert in perfect formation. Retired Air Force Lt. Col. Chris Reymann of Cleveland, Ohio, also piloted UPS aircraft. Reymann has logged more than 4,000 hours in the cockpit. He vividly remembers the Thunderbird tragedy and still knows a thing or two about the importance of aerial support. Reymann supported the U.S. Special Forces, Navy Seals, Delta Force, and various other military and civilian sectors in the 1989 capture of Panamanian Gen. Manuel Noriega. Reymann concurred with the words of Waddell and said, "Without wingmen and teamwork, successful critical missions are impossible."

Aerial wingmen help us better understand the role of spiritual wingmen. The Christian community often refers to wingmen as accountability partners. Using an illustration of God as your commanding officer, you as lead pilot, and your accountability partner as wingman, many spiritual parallels can be drawn. Being a wingman requires faith in the leader and devotion to the cause. Trust is a critical element because you must trust so many to get home safely. The relationship between you and your wingmen often is conducted in dangerous (spiritual) environments. The value of wingmen is best illustrated when the lead pilot experiences spatial disorientation. As believers, we, too, can often be unaware we are flying upside down or straight into the ground. Who but our heavenly commanding officer or a good wingman could spare us from disaster?

Though I am no pilot, I have been fortunate to have had many spiritual wingmen over the years. They have provided me with wise counsel, assisted me in critical decision-making, and pointed me in the right direction.

They had encouraged me, held me up when I was falling, and spared me from danger. Their role in my life has been invaluable. I currently have eight wingmen. That may be too many, but I am fortunate in that most of my wingmen tend to offer a specific specialty in some form, thus the reason for having eight. (I say, the more, the better when going to war.) My wingmen have been carefully chosen and tested over time. They know my strengths and weaknesses. We worship together, pray together, laugh together, and occasionally we cry together (but don't tell anyone). We are transparent with each other. We encourage each other, we serve as sounding boards, we tactfully confront, and we "bust each other's chops." We are brutally honest with each other, and we steal good ideas from each other.

When I have a problem, I try to pray first, and then I go looking for just the right wingman. We watch each other's backs, and we battle Satan together. I certainly don't consult all of them on every issue; too much dissolution of energy, but hardly a week goes by that I don't consult one or more of them for advice. I'm not super-spiritual; I just need a lot of help. We meet in person, we text, we email, and we speak on the phone. We've been known to pray using any one of these communication methods. We have graduated from the barroom to the prayer closet. We share scripture. Wingmen can also be wing women, but most recommend staying within your own gender (except for spouse and family) when it comes to accountability.

We, like pilots, must keep our eyes on the target (Jesus Christ). We must make sure we are following the right leader (Jesus Christ). We must trust our leader and place our faith in Him. We need to also trust our wingmen for guidance and offer some value in return. Wingmen play a critical role in executing the mission laid out by our commanding officer, God. My wingmen do not fly planes, nor do they serve where their physical lives are in danger. They are ordinary guys who are all (and their families) in similar spiritual danger and all searching for the same answers.

They believe in personal responsibility, but they don't believe in flying solo. They are there when you need them. They are available, and they respond without hesitation. Wingmen are good listeners. Wingmen can't always save you, but they often do. Wingmen, hopefully, get stronger together. I believe God often speaks through wingmen. For example, I was recently approached by one of my wingmen, who firmly told me that I was getting too close emotionally too soon to a certain person and that it would take me where I didn't need to be. I bristled at his suggestion until I thought about it for a few days. I later called him and thanked him. I am grateful for my wingmen. Thanks to Hense, Dan, Joe, Derrick, and Jason in Louisville. Thanks to Dean in Murray, Kerry in Paducah, and Alex in Dallas. I salute you and thank you. It's an exciting privilege to share in your adventures and serve alongside you as we all attempt to execute the mission laid out by our commanding officer.

Faith Coach

> "So then, brothers and sisters, stand firm and hold fast to the teachings we passed on to you, whether by word of mouth or by letter."
>
> 2 Thessalonians 2:15

The Murray State University Racers and head coach Steve Prohm are much more than basketball. Yes, they are a perennial powerhouse in the Ohio Valley Conference and a frequent upset winner over larger universities. And yes, the national spotlight further intensified on Murray State when star guard, Isaiah Canaan, was recently named first team all-American. But Prohm said, "We are proud of Isaiah, but he would agree that we build our program around faith—not on individuals." Prohm explains, "The more you get these players in front of faith, the more players like seniors Isaiah and Ed Daniel will have a foundation on which they can build when they leave college. That's our goal—my goal—and the way I think is best to lead."

Lessons from the Bible become the mantra of Prohm teams. Last year, the Racer inspiration came from the book of Nehemiah. When Nehemiah was working to rebuild the walls of Jerusalem, his enemies were angry and felt threatened, so they mocked the project and threatened to harm the workers. Nehemiah continued to build the wall and prayed throughout his project. The enemies tried to distract Nehemiah and demanded he come down off the wall, but Nehemiah and his workers refused. So, the primary theme of last year's Racer team became "Stay on Your Wall. Do not be distracted. There is important work to be done." The Racers wore practice T-shirts monogrammed with "Stay on Your Wall," and they won the OVC Championship and advanced to the NCAA Tournament.

According to Prohm, the 2013 team was built around 1 Corinthians 12:14, "Even so the body is not made up of one part but of many." "Just as Paul said about the church, everyone has a role—the coaches, the players, the managers, the ticket takers, and everyone involved," Prohm said. "Everyone goes hand in hand in achieving one vision and one goal. That really resonates with our players." As for his foundation of faith, Prohm is quick to credit his parents and his predecessor at MSU, Billy Kennedy. Prohm said he was not totally vested in the concept of faith in coaching until he saw Kennedy show the importance of faith when in a position of leadership.

Kennedy worked with Prohm for thirteen years. Kennedy said, "Steve would agree that if you truly believe, then that's a part of who you and your faith naturally flows into basketball." Kennedy added, "Players, for the most part, understand the academic, physical, and mental aspects of the game but few spiritually. That's part of our job."

Neal Bradley of WNBS-FM radio has been the "Voice of the Racers" for over two decades, and he noticed very early that Kennedy emphasized faith. "He carried his Bible on road trips but not for show," Bradley said. "He lived his faith and wanted his players to learn that. Steve Prohm picked right up where Billy Kennedy left off. Both coaches want their players to be better men of faith—not just basketball players." MSU Assistant Athletic Director Dave Winder added, "There's more to life than what happens on the basketball court. Billy Kennedy and Steve Prohm are strong men of faith. They cultivate an environment where that is accepted."

Prohm also has praise for his "accountability" group in Murray. Prohm meets weekly with four men who share their faith and hold each other accountable in matters of integrity. "Once I became a head coach, I knew I had to get further into my faith because I knew I was going to be around young men and have an opportunity to influence them," Prohm said. "I meet with these four men because I know the importance of faith, and I want to be challenged. The idea of Nehemiah came from these men." The faith-based traveling basketball team, Athletes in Action, has also influenced Prohm. He recalled a favorite quote he learned from them: "Do not seek honor. Honor will find you."

Prohm points to Racer forward Stacey Wilson as a living example of that quote. The community of Murray is also a beneficiary of Prohm's public approach to faith. "Murray is a great place to coach basketball and a great place to live. The thing I like about a small college town like Murray is that you get to know people in the community, and they get to know you," Prohm said. "You have the opportunity to help people and the chance to impact the community. This extends to the players, who respond well. They sign every autograph, pose for every photo, and visit all the schools and nursing homes. The people of Murray really look up to them. The players' impact on Murray goes far beyond basketball." Many know Lindy Suiter as the ultimate Racers supporter. Suiter has likely watched Racer basketball, and now Prohm, as closely as anyone. "Coach Prohm is as good as any coach I have seen come through Murray," he said. "His high character attracts high-character players. I've never seen a coach who cares so much about the Murray community."

Billy Kennedy and Steve Prohm have since taken their faith-based coaching approach to larger stages, but MSU continues to reap the benefits of their servant leadership

Barn Church

> "Then your barns will be filled to overflowing,
> and your vats will brim over with new wine."
>
> Proverbs 3:10

Ever worship in a barn? I know one famous guy who did over 2000 years ago. Maybe we all should. Some folks are taking that to heart—like Marshall Fall's family. Yes, they do "regular" church, but his family really loves Barn Church. What is Barn Church? Barn Church is worship with laughter, tears, transparency, hugs, smiles, and never a dull or routine moment. It is worship in unconventional settings where people focus not on the venue or on tradition but on the Lord and those around them who need love.

As far as we know, Barn Church was invented at Barren Heights Retreat Center, which operates on the banks of the Barren River near Bowling Green, KY, and provides respite to families with special-needs children. "We love Barn Church because there is no pressure, and we get to wear what we want," Marshall said. "We love Barn Church because there is no hidden agenda or set schedule. We like to leave room for the Holy Spirit to lead. Often the

Holy Spirit takes us in totally different directions than what we expected. Barn Church is where families love on the Lord and love on each other."

I experienced an incredible Barn Church service that moved one week from the Barn to a ballroom of a Holiday Inn. Why the Holiday Inn? The hotel had hosted a dinner the previous evening to honor special needs children and their families. Some of the families were staying at the hotel and wanted a place to worship, a loving place that could provide for the special needs of special needs families. No problem. Some caring volunteers brought Barn Church to them. This was not your usual worship service. For starters, two large bales of hay were positioned prominently in the front of the ballroom. To the left of the bales sat Marshall, who also serves as the music minister at Amazing Grace Bible Church. He played acoustic guitar and led the group of forty in worship.

The audience consisted of adults and children ranging from newborns to college age. Scripture was read, communion was taken. The Roses, Joe and Toni, founders of Barren Heights, delivered inspiring and touching messages. To offset the rustic barn motif, Joe countered with a fancy PowerPoint presentation. He delivered a heartfelt message about gloves. According to Joe, the hand is like God. The glove is like us, useful only when very close to God. To illustrate the power of transparency, Joe demonstrated the awkwardness of a thick winter glove and the smooth dexterity when using a transparent glove. Even this thick-headed writer could understand that message.

Barn Church that day was home to some of the most natural, heartfelt prayers and testimonies I have ever heard. Yes, I shed tears but don't tell anyone. I also understand that a popular Barn Church tradition is to ask the group: "What is God doing in your life?" The testimonies given surely brought more tears. Toni delivered a moving testimony regarding the previous evening and about loving special needs children and their families. A Barren Heights board member, Ernie Bagley, fought tears when he recounted how the Lord had worked through Barren Heights and Barn Church to greatly touch his family. The framework for supporting these families is Barren Heights.

In the ministry's fledgling years in the mid-2000s, the retreat had a few cottages for special needs families and volunteers. The retreat also had an old barn that no one quite knew what to do with. They tried storing a boat in the barn. They thought about tearing it down because it had housed cows for years, had a bad odor, and was about to fall. The now refurbished barn became a place of worship thanks to the Internal Revenue Service. It seems the IRS was refusing Barren Heights tax-exempt status because they weren't really a "religious" institution.

Joe said, "No problem, we will have a church service for all guests, and we'll have it right over there in the barn! Yeah, that's what we will do. We will have Barn Church! Thank you, IRS." A sheet on the wall became a projector screen. Electricity was run to the barn allowing lights and music. Bales of hay were the pews. Open-air seating had new meaning because the barn was missing doors. One child scrawled scripture on the floor of the upstairs loft. Now the entire interior of the barn is covered in scripture. Talk about being saturated with the Word!

Barn Church has become one of the key features of the Barren Heights weekend retreats. Toni added, "There are so many stories of how God has touched people's lives in Barn Church. One of my favorites was the mom in tears because it was the first time the entire family was able to worship together due to her son's severe disability." Toni also loves the story of the angry man whose heart began to melt in Barn Church. That man eventually was baptized. But Barn Church is so much more than Barren Heights, the Holiday Inn, or the families involved. Barn Church is about a great big God who works in mysterious ways and often uses humble people and odd circumstances to do His work. Since Christ was born in a stable, surely, He smiles when His people worship in a barn. Maybe that's what makes Barn Church special. Or maybe it's the special needs children, which I believe refers to all of us. These are special needs met by a special God.

Warriors for Jesus

> "We are therefore Christ's ambassadors, as though God were making His appeal through us."
>
> 2 Corinthians 5:20

Louisville, KY, is home to a motley crew known as the Warriors. Webster defines motley crew as "an unusually mixed group." A bit of first-hand investigation has proven that definition correct as of the Warriors (as in Warriors for Jesus Christ) are a band of twenty-five or so Christian men who are short or tall, black or white, talkative or shy, married, divorced or single, young or old, educated or not, retired or newly graduated. The Warriors are comprised of financial executives, educators, a pharmacist, a Special Operations Army Ranger veteran, a therapist, a social worker, an IT executive, and other worldly successful men.

But the Warriors are also home to alcoholics, addicts, the near homeless, the physically disabled, the unemployed, the ill, and the financially challenged. So, what bands this motley crew together? The members tell their story best. One of the founders, Jonathan Butcher, said, "People, in general, have a strong desire for community. So, quality groups like the Warriors are important, especially during this season of COVID isolation. The Warrior community offers a safe place for men of all walks of life to share and build friendships, a place where love, trust, truth, and Jesus abound. Jesus was a Warrior too, and we try our best to model Him through prayer and scripture in our meetings and in our daily lives."

Warrior Hense Bennett said, "God designed me for fellowship, and I'm not supposed to navigate this life alone. The Warriors are very valuable to me because they are transparent and trustworthy. The group sticks with the Bible and prayer, keeping the main thing (Jesus) the main thing." These men, who began gathering in March 2020 at the onset of the Coronavirus, welcome Bible newcomers as well as spiritual veterans. They meet via Zoom early every weekday morning with rotating Warriors guiding presentations and discussions on a variety of scriptures and real-life applications. The meetings also regularly feature talks from prominent Christian speakers such as Francis Chan, Tony Evans, Andy Stanley, Bob Russell, and John Piper.

The Warriors stay connected to each other via an app that provides real-time access on their smartphones.

Members frequently post prayer requests, motivating scripture, videos, event updates, and even light-hearted humor. One dedicated Warrior, Karl Bergklint, records and posts an ongoing extensive prayer request list that includes celebration of answered prayer. Early Saturday mornings, the group often gathers for an in-person breakfast followed by prayer. On Sunday morning, many of the Warriors worship together. Chris Dickson said, "I've never seen a group grow to this level of maturity and comradery so quickly. I believe the Holy Spirit must be involved.

The devotion to prayer by these men is intense. I see totally authentic participation in a culture that promotes diversity and sharing in an open and safe setting. I love this group." But the Warriors have a lighter side as well. Laughter and hilarious barbs are frequent. Nicknames are well-deserved, well-received, and worn with honor—the Baconater, Bubbles, Chowder, The Sponge, Sergeant Sprinkles, Mr. Humble, The Brews Brothers, and The Note Taker, to name a few. Warrior Jeff Nally said, "I love to hear and learn from the broad range of perspectives in the group. I especially like hearing the stories of men who are from different backgrounds and in different stages of their faith walk. They all bring value. This diversity has really opened my eyes with stories that inspire, just like the stories of Jesus."

The Warriors apparently don't live only on a virtual Zoom screen. They regularly reach out to those in need. Members, who all chose anonymity on this question, said the group is very active in helping those they encounter who have critical needs, be it spiritually, physically, or financially. All money donated comes from the pockets of the Warriors. Warrior Neil Lovell added this: "I don't say a lot at our meetings. I'm more of a sponge because this group has some amazing biblical knowledge. I am so impressed. It's a fantastic way to start the day. These are wonderful Christian men, and I am very blessed to be a part.

The group must be having an impact because my wife told me to never quit!" Warrior Stephen Woodward also chimed in as he said, "I had been out of church for quite a while but found a good church then the Warriors. I was going through a host of difficulties, but through these men, my relationship with the Lord rejuvenated, and I gained new perspective with Christ as my guiding light for hope and faith." Leader Mark Milburn summed things up when he said, "I think I know the hearts of these men, and they are awesome hearts for Jesus.

The Zoom, for me, is a place where I am always learning, a place where I go to draw nearer to my Savior, and by doing so, I draw nearer to these men because we are all on the same path."

The Serious Jokester

> "Remember your leaders, who spoke the word of God to you. Consider the outcome of their way of life and imitate their faith."
>
> Hebrews 13:7

Ed Anderson loves making people laugh. His jokes are legendary among friends and family. His punchlines are sharp and witty. "Give me a subject, and I'll give you a joke," he said. "If you're down in the dumps, then just tell a joke." Though legally blind and deaf, this ninety-four-year-old World War II veteran and believer in Jesus Christ has never lost his sense of humor. "Despite his challenges, he keeps laughing," said his daughter, Lynn Reid, "I'm not sure I could do that in his situation. Wherever he goes, he is the center of attention because he loves to make people laugh. He's a very funny man. He's a good man with strong faith, values, and morals. Plus, he taught by his actions, not just his words."

"I am a very strong advocate and believer in Jesus," Ed said. "He has covered me my whole life. You gotta have faith. Some of his teachings are very tough, but if you follow them, you're in good shape." Ed's journey through life has not been all jokes. His wife, Mary Leigh, died in 2015. "She was a jewel, a beautiful and good woman. She was a terrific wife and mother. I couldn't ask for anything better," he said. "Before our marriage, I was badly injured in a car accident. I was given last rites. She was my nurse and took great care of me. We became good friends, and when I recovered and left for the service, we corresponded by letter until I came home. I still have those letters today."

The Andersons were married in 1947. Ed credits laughter and faith as the primary reasons for having a marriage that lasted 68 years. Ed joined the U.S. Navy in 1943 at age eighteen. His unit was the first to enter Hiroshima in 1945 after its destruction by an atomic bomb. "The land was scorched; there was not a soul there," he said. Likely exposed to radiation, his unit later managed vessel traffic in Japanese harbors. "But I'm no hero," he said. "I don't deserve any honors." Ed was discharged from the Navy in 1946 with, according to the Navy, severe disabilities.

Growing up in Louisville was not easy for Ed. His parents divorced when he was five, and he was raised by his mother, who taught him to put God first. He worked seven days a week at a grocery store while in high school.

He made twenty-two dollars a week and gave his mother eighteen dollars of his pay. While in the Navy, Ed made seventy-five dollars a month and sent sixty dollars home to his mother. "I had no money to join the boys for a social life," Ed said. "Kids today are spoiled. They get everything they want." As a husband and parent, Ed rode streetcars to school and work while raising six children with Mary Leigh. Taking college classes mostly at night, he graduated from the University of Louisville.

In his professional career, Ed worked for the Army Corp of Engineers, the Internal Revenue Service, and the Veteran's Administration before using his finance expertise to run his own business. Today, Ed lives in East Louisville with his son, Kevin, who serves as his primary caregiver. "Like any father-son relationship, it's trying, at times, but we mostly get along great," Kevin said. "This experience has taught me patience, tolerance, and understanding. Dad taught us the value of hard work. That work ethic turned out to be valuable in our professional careers. Any big or small problem, he has always been here to listen and help in any way he can, and, of course, both of my parents led by their faith."

Gary, the youngest Anderson son, said, "Over the years, the thing that sticks with me most about my dad is his solid, firm commitment to his family. He was always striving to do the right thing. He is certainly a man of integrity. He never spoke a lot about religion; he just lived his faith and instilled the right values in his children. He worked long hours, and sometimes the money was tight, but he always said that even in adversity, if you stick to your principles and values, you'll be alright."

These days, with the help of a magnifying device, Ed enjoys analyzing and organizing his coin and stamp collections. He said he would leave them to his eleven grandchildren and seven great-grandchildren, not just for the monetary value but in hopes that the hobby would draw them closer together after he was gone.

"Jesus has been with me my entire life," Ed said. "I pray a simple prayer every night. I thank God I was able to take care of my wife and children. I pray that I will have no pain and that it will happen soon. I'm ready to go."

Ed Anderson joined Mary Leigh in heaven in 2020.

FAMILY FIRST

> "For the sake of my family and friends, I will say, 'Peace be within you.'"
>
> Psalm 122:8

When Dad died in 2011, the family estate was left entirely to Mom. When Mom died in 2018, the estate was willed to their seven children to be distributed in equal portions. My sister B and I were tasked with managing the legal affairs. When we met with the estate attorney, B said, "Just divide it equally in seven portions and draw up the papers. Everyone will review and sign. There will be no issues." The attorney simply agreed, but later, he confessed that he laughed to himself because few estates are settled without conflict, let alone one with seven recipients. There has not been a conflict to this day. That event is so characteristic of our family. I credit Mom and Dad for establishing that harmony and my brothers and sisters for remaining true to their heritage. Someone in the family said, "All families love each other to one degree or another. This is much more intense." Generations to come will reap the benefits. After our Lord, it's always family first.

Mom

"We are conquerors, not quitters."

Alta Hinkle

My mother, Alta Mae Hinkle, loved Jesus Christ, and she loved her Bible. She lived a joyful life and was faithful to Christ despite the numerous challenges she faced in eighty-nine years of living. My parents raised seven children, one with a traumatic brain injury. They also cared for, in our home, Mom's aging and ill parents. So, counting Dad, Richard Hinkle, that made eleven of us at the supper table every night. Of course, Mom did all the cooking. All of this took place in a small, rural Kentucky farmhouse with only four bedrooms and no air conditioning. We had no shower, just a bathtub. Mom worked the farm with all of us. We raised tobacco, cattle, horses, and vegetables.

Dad had two other jobs to support the family. Mom was tasked with farm work, shopping, cooking, laundry, doctor visits, homework, school events, ballgames, sewing, bookkeeping, housekeeping, caring for neighbors, Bible study, and more—for many years. Through it all, she lavished us with love. But far above the demands of daily life, Mom insisted the entire family, unfailingly, go to church three times a week—Sunday morning, Sunday evening, and Wednesday evening. Crops, ballgames, and school activities could wait. Walt Disney and The Wizard of Oz (Sunday night television) could wait too. Snow and rare vacations were no excuse for missing church. Worship always came first. Mom believed in and was forever dedicated to her Lord and Savior, Jesus Christ, to prayer, her Bible, her family, her friends, and her church.

She and Dad were loyal to each other through fifty-nine years of marriage. Mom's faithfulness paid huge dividends as the storms of life raged. Hard work, medical dilemmas, financial challenges, a severely injured son, and many other battles faced the Hinkle family. Perhaps the most amazing aspect of this era was that the family was happy. We didn't know we were poor. We laughed. We had fun. The Hinkle story is not all challenges. Our home was always full of Bibles—Bibles that were read by all, not just books sitting on a shelf. Mom read the Bible to us and taught us how to read it ourselves. Mom taught children's Bible classes for years.

She was well known for her hand-written cards of encouragement. Her home was a frequent stop for

Christian women—many of whom she mentored, and yes, into her eighties, she always went to church three times a week until she couldn't. Even then, she had communion brought to her hospital bed. She read her Bible until she couldn't, then she had someone read it to her. She read her devotionals until she couldn't, then she had someone read them to her. The devotional writing below was one of her favorites. This well summarizes her attitude toward life:

> "I am confident in my Lord. I have a victorious attitude. I am one of God's most prized possessions. God turns disappointments into appointments. There is only one safe place to be in this world—in the arms of Jesus. I will rise and be successful, I am more than a conqueror—not a quitter.
>
> I am confident in my Lord. My inner being is renewed day by day. I have hope that something good is going to happen because I expect the best. I have a victorious attitude. I am a conqueror, not a quitter. He loves me, and I am highly favored because with God all things are possible."
>
> Author unknown

A laminated copy of these words was found in her Bible. Mom was indeed a conqueror, not a quitter—the same as Dad. They instilled these powerful lessons into seven children, seventeen grandchildren, and four great-grandchildren—all believers.

Mom and Dad lived life the right way—God's way.

Dad

"They're my family, I'll take care of them."

Richard Hinkle

My father, Richard Hinkle, was ten feet tall, bulletproof, fearless, the strongest man in the world, an intellectual genius, and as great a Christian as Billy Graham. Or so it seemed when I was ten years old. Some Saturday mornings, we spent time together just he and I. Those times were awesome. I watched him carefully so that I could mimic his every move. He was my hero. We drove to town to run errands. Dad was always fun-loving but humble.

Everyone in town knew him. They smiled, waved, and stopped to talk. They sought him for advice. They liked and respected him. They liked me too—because I was his son. Maybe they liked him for his humor. Maybe they admired him for his integrity—always telling the truth and paying his bills on time. Or maybe, they respected him for his work ethic. Dad worked forty years as a security guard, then chemist at the Union Carbide Uranium Enrichment Plant. After eight hours at the plant, Dad worked on our farm, raising cattle, horses, tobacco, and commercial vegetables. In the wee hours of the morning, he would rise to deliver newspapers to most all of the county. He then would sleep two hours before going to the plant again.

There seemed to be no end to his drive to provide for his family. Dad was no stranger to adversity. His eldest son was critically injured in a car accident and severely disabled for life. He endured crop failures, financial hardship, and steep medical challenges of his own. Through it all, he demonstrated his trademark grit, determination, and perseverance. He was a man's man, in every sense of the word. The demands were intense, providing for a wife, seven children, and my Mom's aging parents. Despite the long work hours, Dad always made time for us in laughing, joking, and playing games. He loved us so much. We all felt like we were his favorite child.

Dad was a quiet spiritual giant. He loved Jesus Christ. He prayed, studied his Bible, and taught his children right versus wrong. He was a loving and devoted son, brother, husband, father, grandfather, uncle, and friend. He never spoke much about spiritual matters; he just lived them. He was obedient and tough as nails. His life flowed with the fruit of the Spirit—love, joy, peace, patience, kindness, goodness, faithfulness, gentleness, and self-control.

In retirement, Dad hardly retired. He traveled with Mom. He transported vehicles across the country. He served, at his new church in town, as deacon and a handyman for the church and the members. If someone needed something done, Dad was always there. He could seemingly fix anything. He served on mission trips. He was a gardener, bird watcher, and woodworker who created incredible works of art. He loved puzzles of all types; he flew remote control planes, went to college, and enjoyed his laptop computer. His home was full of books. He was an inquisitive man who never stopped learning.

Dad and Mom were married for fifty-nine years. When Dad died in 2011, at the age of eighty-two, his memorial service was packed. The line of people stretched throughout the church and out into the street. They were there to honor a man they greatly respected. I heard amazing stories from people who would recount what Dad had done for them. I had never heard most of these stories. Dad wasn't one to talk about such. One hometown friend reported that the Town Council, respecting Dad's integrity and work ethic, once offered Dad a financial donation when we were going through a tough time. Dad said, "They're my family; I'll take care of them."

He said all seven of his children would have a chance

to go to college. They did. A line I recall from his service was, "I'd rather see a sermon than hear a sermon." That was Dad. I invited him many times to Men's Ministry events at my church. He always declined, and finally, he said, "I'd rather do something than just talk about it." Again, that was Dad. When he was near death, I asked him if he was afraid to die. He said he was. I was shocked, given the fearless life he had lived and his strong faith. So, I asked him why. He smiled and responded, "I've never done this before!" Classic Dad to the very end.

Dad and Mom lived life the right way—God's way.

Four Sisters

> "And now these three remain: faith, hope and love. But the greatest of these is love."
>
> 1 Corinthians 13:13

Few have four sisters. I do. A trip down memory lane reveals mostly humor from our childhood days. A highlight was the "battle for the bathroom." The battle was fierce since we grew up in a small farmhouse with two grandparents, two parents, four girls, three boys, and one bathroom. Yes, that's correct. One bathroom. I had to be creative to weasel my way into the bathroom, especially when my teenage sisters were preparing for dates. My knocking on the bathroom door was incessant and usually ignored. The only positive from the dilemma was that I learned to joyfully utilize the backyard for relieving nature's call.

I learned a trick, however, that often solved the bathroom problem. I discovered that our phone (rotary) could be made to ring itself. I always answered those calls and announced through the closed bathroom door that a boyfriend was calling. When they hurried, in their bathrobe, to a silent phone, I would dash into the bathroom, lock the door, and enjoy a luxurious, hot bath—laughing all the time. The only sound I could hear was the sister wailing loudly, "Mom!!! Dad!!!!" My laughter increased. Yes, I tortured my sisters. I drove them crazy. I had them running from my tomato, rock, and corn cob hurling. I told, after dark, scary and somewhat believable stories about monsters in the yard, skeletons in the barn, creatures in the garage, and a dead man hanging in the old apple tree.

I totally antagonized their boyfriends. I told the boys outrageously embarrassing and sometimes true stories. I let air out of their tires. I followed them when they left on dates. But alas, the torture was not one-sided. My pride will not allow me to tell all tales, but I will share one particularly painful story. I was surprise-attacked by all four sisters and tied firmly, with a thick rope, to the base of a giant oak tree in the front yard. Then, in the heat of the summer, with the hot sun glaring down upon me, they wrapped many thick wool blankets around me until only my head was exposed. As if that were not enough, they dripped freezing cold water from a tin cup on my nose. They left me to suffer. Finally, rescue arrived. My Dad walked up, surveyed the situation, and calmly said, "You probably deserved this." He turned and walked away.

Mercifully for all, college came, and we went our separate ways. Oddly enough, our bonds grew much closer as time went by and distance increased. Holidays together became incredibly sweet. "I love you" and hugs became standard fare. We all watched in admiration as careers blossomed. My oldest sister is a highly respected school psychologist testing specialist. My second sister crafted a very successful career as a nurse practitioner, then corporate vice president. My third sister is a trusted finance manager and earned perhaps the highest honor by raising, as a single parent, five college graduates. My fourth sister is a talented and dedicated nurse manager at a major hospital, valiantly leading her nurses on the front lines of COVID treatment.

But these incredible women have accomplishments that go far beyond professional careers. Between the five of us, we have raised seventeen extraordinarily successful children. I'm not sure how all that happened. But it did. And it's not over. Perhaps the most impressive attribute of my sisters is that they are all followers of Jesus Christ. They raise Believing children, they pray, they read their Bibles, they serve with other Christian women, they attend church, and they sing—very well! They bear and share the fruits of the Holy Spirit. They walk their talk.

They give of their money, time, and energy to those in need—usually anonymously. They nurture their children in biblical truth. They lovingly cared for our dying parents. They live for others, not themselves.

But as the famous song "My Old Kentucky Home" goes, "by and by, hard times come a knocking at the door." Such was the case for the five of us. We endured dark seasons of divorce, medical dilemmas, financial challenges, child catastrophe, aging parents, and very tough decisions. We leaned on each other; we cried together, we prayed together, and then we strategized. We ultimately rose to thrive above the adversity. We did it together, and we bonded even closer.

But did I mention that my sisters are fun? I really enjoy being with them. We have worked together and vacationed together. We make fun of each other, and we play practical jokes. But no more tomatoes, rocks, corn cobs, or wool blankets. We have graduated from rotary phone to smiley faces on a smartphone. Though we are far apart geographically, rarely a day goes by without at least a text. We love to smile. We laugh loudly. They have helped me immensely. Maybe I have helped them a bit. How could such love and legacy grow from a large family in a tiny farmhouse in rural Kentucky? I'm not sure.

In fact, I am amazed. Jesus Christ and our parents are indeed primarily responsible. But I certainly give much credit to my sisters. I don't fully understand how all of this happened. But one thing I do know is that I love my sisters, and they love me. I am a very lucky man.

Dedicated to B, Cara, Jo, and Annie

A Tortured Believer

> "I have told you these things, so that in Me you may have peace. In this world you will have trouble. But take heart! I have overcome the world."
>
> John 16:33

Some say a long-time Christian probably walks with a bit of a limp because of the trials they have endured. If so, Hadi may limp his way right into heaven. Hadi came to the USA from Iran as a Muslim in 1976 and was baptized into Christianity in 1984. In 1985, he returned to Iran to care for his ailing mother. He had no idea what lay in store for him. The Secret Police of Tehran were not pleased to hear of Hadi's enthusiasm for evangelizing to Muslims, so they began to threaten him on a regular basis. He was not allowed to leave the country. Leaving his mining job one day, Hadi was nabbed by the fanatic guards, whipped with lashes, and tossed into a forty-foot-deep mining shaft known for being the home of tarantulas and poisonous snakes. He suffered a broken hip and shattered leg in the fall and would pass in and out of consciousness for seven hours lying on the dark cave floor. While lucid, Hadi prayed for survival. He said he felt the presence of Christ.

Finally, a passing foreman heard his screams and rescued him for a ten-hour surgery that left his left leg shorter forever. Throughout, he remained an ardent Christian, especially because he believed God had spared him from the pit. Hadi would return to the USA in 2002 after again being threatened with death in Iran. He thrived as a free Christian, married in 2006, and became a permanent USA resident in 2011. Hadi often shares his faith with groups, including Bible classes. He said, "I don't believe anything about Islam. Christ is the one for me. Being a Christian is the biggest thing that happened in my life because I know that my sins are forgiven. I would be dead had I not left Iran. My experiences have made my faith stronger. Now nothing would make me deny Christ. Christ is the answer for the rest of the world and the only hope for peace for everyone, especially those in the Middle East."

In 2007 Hadi was joined by his teenage son Joseph who was also freed from Iran. Hadi says that in addition to enjoying his son, he was able to show him Christ and how to live in a free world without pressure and not be brainwashed by Muslim fanatics. Joseph was baptized into Jesus Christ in 2009. Joseph said, "At first, I was most excited to see Dad. I missed him badly, but the more

I live here, the more I appreciate America, Christianity, and freedom. I always dreamed of coming here and always had hopes, but you never know, so now it is all very joyous for me. The Muslim people in Iran are so oppressed, so I moved away from religion while there, but here, I found Christianity to be so much more liberal and freeing. The freedom of Christianity is great."

Lisa, also a believer, is the wife of Hadi and the stepmother of Joseph. She said. "In addition to what Hadi means to me, it is amazing how one man's life has had such a dramatic Christian influence on both Christians and Muslims. Joseph is a talented young man who we are very proud of. Along with our Christian daughter Haley, he makes our family complete." Rising beyond adversity, Hadi continues his bold walk. For the entire family, limping is now considered a high honor.

God Spoke

"One thing God has spoken,
two things I have heard:
"Power belongs to you, God,
and with you, Lord, is unfailing love";
and, "You reward everyone
according to what they have done.

Psalm 62:11

The horrific crash took mere seconds to occur. My SUV had, according to witnesses, hit pooled water on the interstate, hydroplaned, turned two circles, left the highway, slammed into an embankment, rolled twice, and landed upright. I sat dazed, still strapped into my seatbelt. The air had an odd smell, and strange noises came from the engine. The windshield was gone. Airbags had deployed. The inside of the SUV looked like a tornado had struck. I searched for blood and found none. I checked to see if my body parts were intact. They were. I had no pain. My thinking seemed to be reasonably clear.

As best I could tell, I didn't have even a scratch. My good luck had begun. While I waited for help, I'd like to say I prayed intense thanks for survival. But I didn't. My mind just swirled rapidly through a flood of thoughts. I wondered if I was in heaven. I envisioned my children, family, and friends. I thought, What in the world just happened? In my daze, I would not have been surprised to see a Scarecrow, a Tin Man, and a Cowardly Lion. Two angels, cleverly disguised as men in pick-up trucks, hurriedly arrived to offer their assistance.

Once they determined that I was apparently okay physically, we talked. I remember one saying, "We saw what happened. How did you survive that? You are one lucky dude." They called 911, tended to me, and then began a search, in the rain, for my valuables, which were scattered in a wide radius. Shortly thereafter, they returned with my wallet, eyeglasses, two cellphones, a laptop, and a briefcase—all perfectly intact. The good luck was now a little scary. I wish I had the names of those two angels who disappeared too soon.

The State Police Officer and the paramedics were equally incredulous. The officer said he had seen many much less violent crashes where the driver did not survive. He called me a very lucky man. The paramedics could hardly believe I had no injuries. They, too, said I was a very lucky man. The only issue they had was my elevated blood pressure. We laughed about that. They offered to take me to the hospital for further checks. I declined. I was perfectly fine. I am perfectly fine today. They told me I would be very sore in the morning. I was not.

The officer suggested that I sit in the backseat of his car to relax until the tow truck arrived. He then found a large drink cup and began gathering, in the rain, a significant amount of spare change that had spilled from the vehicle. After quite a while, he gave me the cup and even some paper money he found. I don't believe coin collecting is in his job description. He took good care of me. I evidently was indeed lucky. While waiting alone, in the backseat of a state police cruiser, the whole point of this story played out. God spoke to me. He did not speak in an audible voice, but the mental impression was undeniable. The message cut right to my heart. God spoke three simple sentences to me. "Walk closer to Me than ever before. Listen more intently to Me than ever before. Do what you are told." The words ran through my mind over and over, for the next few hours, for the next few days and weeks, and even today.

I never had to write them down. They are emblazoned in my mind and heart. I will never forget them. I tell others the story. Some are impressed; others write it off as some sort of imaginary post-accident trauma. That's fine. I'll keep believing, and I'll keep telling the story. I wish I could say that since the accident, I have followed those directions perfectly. But I have not. I'm trying and getting better. I will continue to. Why did God speak to me? I'm not sure. What I do suspect is that there was more than "luck" at play in this event. What is the meaning of the three sentences? To me, the meaning is self-explanatory. But the words also have a ring of mystery. I believe more will be revealed. All I know for sure is that I am alive and that God spoke to me on the side of that interstate. I believe that without a doubt, and I'm doing my best to follow the instructions.

> "Walk closer to me than ever before.
> Listen more intently to me than ever before.
> Do what you are told."

Our Kids Are Crazy, Too!

> "Children are a heritage from the Lord,
> offspring a reward from Him."
>
> Psalm 127:3

We are blessed with three incredible and beautiful children. They are over-achievers spiritually, mentally, physically, socially, athletically, academically, and professionally. Olivia, twenty-two, is a ministry leader and married to Jackson, a recent triple major college graduate on the fast track to success. Emory, nineteen, our second daughter, is excelling at a major university where she too is a ministry leader. Our youngest, Asa, is seventeen and in high school. He is a superstar at church, school, girls, and baseball. All three have a wonderful sense of humor, but perhaps none compared to when they were much younger.

When little ones say something funny or cute, an adult will often say, "You should write that down." Well, I did. The following pages are actual notes and quotes that were written and saved from when the kids were roughly the ages of two (Asa), four (Emory), and seven (Olivia). Most characters in these conversations are (except family) totally imaginary in the minds of these creative kids. Enjoy!

—

Elderly woman looks lovingly at Olivia and says, "When you get married, will I get an invitation to your wedding?"

Olivia, "Sure, if you're still alive."

—

As I clean the kitchen, Olivia walks in dressed like Princess Di (in her mind). She looks a little floozy in her dress-up finest—glittering mini-skirt, pink top with straps, plastic high heels, and a ton of play make-up. I managed to keep a straight face, and we have the following conversation—dead serious, not even a smile.

"Hi, Olivia. Watcha doin'?"

"Going on a date."

"With who?"

(with annoyed expression) "John, of course! Who else?"

"Oh, where you going to eat?"

"Well, first we're going to Shake N Steak—but not the one you know about. It's another one where they have a dance floor."

"Oh, so you're going to eat some hamburgers and do some dancing?"

"Yeah, probably a lot of dancing. Then we're going to the mall. John needs some new shoes, and the flowers came off my heels, so I need to find more."

"Hey, Olivia, I was just wondering. Is John a good driver?

Because I don't want you riding with someone unless they're very safe."

(annoyed again) "Dad! I always drive. You know John is younger than me. He doesn't have a driver's license yet."

Ten minutes later, after dancing alone to the stereo, Olivia returns to the kitchen and says, "Dad, don't worry if John kisses me because we are already engaged and know we are going to get married."

—

"Want sum more of that Q Bar."

It took us a few hours to figure out Emory wanted more of the BBQ we had a few days prior.

—

Emory sitting on her little throne,

Me, "Emory, did you do anything?"

Emory, "Naw, just a couple toots."

—

Olivia and I have been studying a children's guide to Jesus. We read a little, and then we talk about it.

"Olivia, tell me what heaven is."

"Well, that's where Jesus lives with God, and it's where Christians get to go live when they die. If people aren't good, then they, well, it's like the Tom and Jerry cartoon when Tom got hit by the piano and was killed. He walked up some steps to heaven, but he had to get a contract signed saying he was forgiven for all the bad things he did. But Jerry would not sign it because Tom had always been very mean to Jerry and still was. There was a big clock ticking, and when it ran out, Tom fell through a trap door into a pot of boiling water—way down in a cave where the devil lives. But I saw Tom later, on another cartoon, so he must have woken up from a dream-like Dorothy on the Wizard of Oz."

—

Last Saturday, we treated Mom to a day off alone for shopping. While she was gone, we cleaned the bathroom. While we were cleaning, Olivia said:

"Mama's going to be so happy. I think we should give her a day off every January."

—

I called home from afar and was talking with Emory. "I'll be back tomorrow!"

"Will you please come to my house?"

—

Fallout from Sunday's honoring of senior citizens on the church stage:

On the way to school today, Olivia and I passed a cemetery. "Did you bury Grandma Clossie there?"

"No, she was buried in her town.

"Will you take me there sometime?"

"Yes."

"How did she die?"

"She was very old, and one day she didn't wake up. She went to heaven."

"How did you know she had died?"

"She wasn't breathing. But don't worry, that only happens to very old people. Clossie would be well over a hundred years old if she were alive today."

"Boy, they would have really clapped loud for her at church yesterday, wouldn't they?"

—

"Emory, tell your mother what happened at Olivia's soccer practice."

"I pee-peed in the chair."

"Why did you do that?"

"I dunno."

"What happened after that?"

"A little boy sat in it."

"What did you say?"

"Holy cow!"

—

Daddy and Emory at bedtime.

"Emory, what kind of story do you want tonight?"

"Story about Emory, Daddy, and a mean giraffe."

—

Whenever you are caught doing something bad, try Emory's technique. Smile and say,

"Just betending."

—

Emory, "What are you doing, Daddy?"

"Putting medicine on my tail."

"Is it sore?"

"Yes."

"Does it have red spots?"

"I don't know."

"Can I see it?"

"No."

"I will pray to Jesus to make it all better."

—

I was growing a mustache and goatee. Our master bed is very high off the floor. Today, I lay exhausted on the bed and saw Emory enter the bedroom. Though I could not see the top of her head to the left of my bedside, I saw a Brillo pad come flying over me and onto the covers, and then a toothbrush and then a surgical glove, and then another surgical glove.

She yelled to be lifted up, which I did. I sat her beside me and asked, "What are you doing?"

She replied, "I'm here to work on your whiskers."

—

I was working in the yard today, wearing only gym shorts and tennis shoes. Emory came onto the porch with hands on her hips and a scowl on her face.

"Why are you mowing necked?"

—

Olivia fell roller skating yesterday—five stitches underneath her chin.

Emory wants some stitches, too.

—

Last night's game on the back deck was orchestrated by Olivia, with everyone in character for a pretend event.

Olivia—Cinderella

Emory—Snow White

Asa—baby Moses

Mom—the mean stepmother who made them all do chores

—

While working in my office this morning, Olivia arrived in breathless excitement and announced, "Daddy, it's a dream come true! I'm going to Paris. Teresa's parents are taking her, and they have extra tickets. So, me, Dodi, Macey, Ginger, and Lilly are going, too. We're going for four days, so I'll miss a little school. We might meet some cute boys. Do you have a camera I can borrow?"

—

Olivia comforts Emory after Olivia was chosen to play her video games first.

"Just remember, Emory, the Bible says the first shall be last, and the last shall be first. So, you'll get to go to heaven first."

—

Last night I was massaging Emory's legs.

"Daddy, tell me I have pretty legs."

"You do."

"No, say it."

—

Emory singing (before she was chosen to go to heaven first) Sung to the tune of "Skip to My Lou."

"Kip, kip, kip to the moon.
Kip to the moon, my darling."

—

My office at home is now a fully functioning schoolhouse classroom with teacher (Olivia) and twenty-three students (Emory and twenty-two stuffed animals) sitting at their desks.

This conversation was overheard last night:

Olivia, "Okay, class, who can tell me? What is two plus two?"

Emory, "One!"

Olivia, "No."

Emory, "Two!"

Olivia, "No."

Emory, "Free!"

Olivia, "No."

Emory, "Four!"

Olivia, "Good. Now, the next question."

—

Emory's new routine before going to sleep—prayer, then place breakfast order.

Last night, "Amen. Daddy, I want a pop-tart, waffles, and pancakes for breakfast."

—

Leaving the girls' bedroom after tucking them in.

Emory, "Daddy, wait! You didn't take breakfast orders!"

Dad, "Okay, what do you want?"

Emory, "I'll have oatmeal, toast with butter, a cinnamon roll, orange juice, milk, and coffee."

Olivia, "That sounds good. I'll have that, too."

—

Emory's two new favorite words—guaranteed to get a belly laugh from her at the mere mention:
Boogeyman and stink bug.

—

"Daddy, I have chosen everyone for my wedding. Emory will be my maid of honor. Natalie, Rachel, and Kayla will be bridesmaids. But I'll have to have a talk with Kayla because she will probably want to do something silly."

Dad, "Can I be in the wedding?"

Olivia, "Silly Daddy. There are no bride's boys!"

—

After a couple of holes in our annual golf tournament, I noticed Olivia had a non-stop scowl on her face and was very quiet. Leaving the green and heading back to the cart, I whispered in her ear—"You better turn that attitude around."

She replied, "Daddy, I don't have a bad attitude. It's like when you're not talking sometimes when we are in the car. This is my concentration face. I really want to win."

—

Our family Memorial Day Weekend 2005:

Stayed up late
Slept late
Watched movies—Bambi, Barney, Olsen twins
Sponge Bob Marathon
COPS Marathon
Ate watermelon
Read books
Went for walks
Chased geese
Ate anything we wanted
Planted flowers
Planted tree
Went to church
Had a cookout
Played video games
Girls went shoe shopping while boys watched
baseball
Took naps
Took Asa for stroller rides
Lots of time on swing
Ride in the Jeep with everyone in the front seat
Played tee-ball
Went for ice cream
Went fishing—caught six
Played all our favorite games—Monkey in the Middle,
Monster on the Playground, Snake Hole, I Don't Think So,
and Challenge

—

A conversation on the way to church:

"Emory, did you go to Isabel's house this morning?"

"Yes."

"Did you cross the street?"

"Yes."

"Did you ask me before you went?"

"No."

"Did you look both ways?"

"No, but don't worry, Daddy, I'll just do it when we get back home. I promise."

—

Emory: "Daddy, I'm going to lay down and rest. Wake me up at twenty o'clock."

—

Olivia, "Mama, from now on, I want a list of chores every day because I love to help out."

Mom, "Sure, we can make that happen."

Olivia, "But I'll still need some free time for myself because I don't want to be like you or anything."

—

Emory, "Daddy, when we go to the beach again, don't worry about the sharks because I learned all about them in school, and I can protect the family."

"Well, how do you know if sharks are in the area?"

Emory, "You can see their beak above the water."

—

Olivia, "Daddy, I can figure skate."

Emory, "Daddy, I can figure skate, too."

Olivia, "You cannot."

Emory, "I can too."

Olivia, "You can't."

Emory, "Can, too."

Olivia, "Fine, then show me a triple-double higgleberry." Later she demanded Emory do "The Flying Shrimp."

After dark, Olivia came into the house with a scrape down the side of her face. I asked her what happened. She told me, "Never figure skate in the dark on the sidewalk."

"Honey, what did you hit?"

"My face."

—

Olivia and John have decided to get married while we are on vacation. Here are a few of the emerging details:

Natalie will be the maid of honor.

Erin, Molly, Lauren, Heather, Haley, Holly, Hannah, and Ana Sofia are in the running for bridesmaid slots.

Emory will not be in the wedding
(as of today—something about a coloring book).

John is studying to be a dentist.
Olivia is a veterinarian.

They will live with us for a while.

John's father is a jewel master.

Cara (violin), Ella (clarinet), and Annie (drums) are in the running for musician slots, but the favorites at this point are Aunt B on piano and Nicolas on guitar.

—

After taking communion today, Emory asked in a loud voice,

"Why dat man give you a snack?"

—

7 a.m.:

Dad, "Emory, want something to eat?"

Emory, "Yeah, breakfast."

—

Olivia, "Emory! A wild dog got into the kitchen and ate all our food!"

With a terrified face, she runs into the kitchen and returns with a package of crackers. "No, he didn't, Daddy—see!"

—

We have various names for Asa:

Jackson
Richard
Chunk
Hoss
Smiley
AJ
Bruiser
Bean Boy
Smilin' Jack
Ol' Blue Eyes
Adventure Boy
Hammerhead
AJ the Blue Jay
Little Fella
Big Guy
Junior Calloway
Acey
Tater
Little Davey Boy
Einstein
Hambone

—

Dad, "Emory, what do you want for breakfast?"

Emory, "Big bowl, Fruit Loops, milk, and a poon."

Dad, "It's a s-s-s-s-spoon."

Emory, "I like poon better."

—

Olivia had a baby this morning, Blake Jonathan Hinkle; all are well.

Oddly enough, Emory had a baby shortly after Olivia's announcement, Taylor—a baby girl.

...

Sad news regarding Olivia's new baby.

Olivia informed us that Jonathan Blake died this morning. Seems that after having some bad behavior, Jonathan was placed in time-out, but he escaped by driving off in the Barbie car. Olivia found him dead in the kitchen, where he had been playing with knives and apparently stabbed himself. Despite his bad behavior, Olivia says he was a pretty good kid. She just hopes her next kid is better behaved.

Emory just announced that her baby died, too.

—

If you haven't noticed, Emory loves to eat—nonstop.

Thus, her nickname is "Snacky."

—

In conversation, Aunt B mentioned to Emory that her daddy is very smart. She matter-of-factly replied,

"He certainly is. He knows all of his numbers and most of his colors."

—

Olivia's best lines from vacation.

After smooth-talking Emory into doing something funny, Olivia said, "I just love the way I use words."

...

Halfway home, Olivia announced that she would take a nap. Mom asked if Olivia wanted Patti (her favorite doll). Olivia said, "No, and if Patti needs me, tell her I'm unavailable."

—

Olivia, having lost her first tooth, raised some suspicions about the reality of a tooth fairy. We answered in vague general terms that left open the possibility.

Yesterday, she lost her second tooth, and the tooth fairy visited again. While on business travel, I called, and she expressed supreme confidence in the existence of said fairy because:

"Dad was out of town when fairy visited. And Mom would NEVER lie to me."

...

After our tooth fairy discussion, I asked Olivia what she was doing. "I'm tutoring Emory. She really needs help with math and numbers."

Then I got on the phone with Emory and asked what she was doing. "Olivia is tooting me, but I don't like it."

Later, I learned from Mom that Olivia had attempted to deprive Emory of food and water until she exhibited progress.

—

Olivia came up to me at church and whispered angrily in my ear, "This dress Mom made me wear is humiliating. It looks like something a four-year-old would wear. The collar is hideous. I am not happy."

—

Emory loses scissor privileges:

Dad, "Emory, why did you cut off some of Olivia's hair?"

Emory, "We were playing Booty Parlor, so I was cuttin' hair."

Olivia, "Hey, they don't call it cuttin' for nothin'!"

—

Emory, quite indignant, enters the room and announces, "Livia says I'm a loser. I'm *not* a loser."

A handwritten note was found in Emory's hand:

Did not pass. try again next time.
love, coach Olivia

—

Whispering from Emory overheard as she went stomping up the stairs:

"Dear Jesus. Please help Daddy have better behavior. Amen, Jesus."

—

From the water park:

Olivia, six, takes off to explore a giant water playground while I sit nearby and return some phone messages.

"Now, Olivia, I will be right here. Play all you want but do not leave this area."

"Dad, why would I leave this area? You think I want to get lost or kidnapped or something? Besides, you have all the money."

—

I will spare you the details but will share with you some quotes from Olivia's teacher regarding Olivia's performance:

"A pleasure to teach."
"A beautiful child."
"A great memory for stories and scripture."
"Wonderfully self-motivated."
"A great student."
"A helper and encourager of others."
"Outstanding in every category."
"She must have truly incredible parents—especially the father!"

Maybe I made one up.

—

Woke early Sunday am and was making my way, bleary-eyed, to the coffeepot. I passed the living room where Emory was asleep (?) on the couch. Heard a voice say,

"Morning, Monkey Butt!"

—

Asa-Antics:

Wander around the house looking for something dangerous, then grab it and run like crazy.

Wait until Olivia or Emory build something, then destroy it.

Sit on my butt and slam my forehead into the floor repeatedly until I get what I want.

Follow Emory around the house and beg for crumbs.

Dive headfirst into anything just to see what happens.

Find something new to hit Emory on the head with—preferably heavy.

Unplug every electrical device and pull the cord very hard to see what happens.

Wander aimlessly around the house, looking for things that can potentially make a lot of noise.

New Names—Destructo, Hoss, the Walking Terror

—

Tonight, Emory told me a bedtime story. It was about Winnie the Pooh fighting the Canaanites.

—

Driving home from school yesterday:

Olivia, "Can I still go to the roller-skating party tonight?"

Dad, "Yes."

Olivia, "Are you still going with me instead of Mom?"

Dad, "Yes, Mom has a meeting. Is that okay?"

Olivia, "Yes."

Dad, "You know, Mom is a very good skater. What if I'm not very good at skating? Is that still okay?"

Olivia, "I haven't had that discussion in my mind yet."

—

Emory is taking her two (imaginary) boyfriends to school today—Peter and James.

—

Last night Emory wanted me to tell a story that included her, Barney, Silly Billy, and an ol' mean nasty gorilla.

—

"Wivia! I got two things to you to we-member.Number one. I'm in charge. Number two. I'm the Boss."

—

Me and the three kids playing golf in the front yard last night:

Olivia, "While working on her swing, "Don't talk to me right now. It disconcentrates me."

Emory, after waving to the neighbor, "Now I have to start all over again. Does everyone have to wave at me?"

Asa—inserts tee into ground, removes tee, eats dirt off tee.

—

Our family conversation before walking into church yesterday:

Emory, "They might tell me I look pretty or have a pretty dress or have a pretty mouth."

Olivia, "No, you only say pretty mouth when you are in love."

Emory turns and points to a spot in lawn—"Is that poop?"

—

Emory's two imaginary boyfriends' (Peter and James) parents were killed.

They lived in a tree at the park across the street but spent a lot of time at our house.

—

Emory is reading a book when she should have been getting dressed.

Dad, "Emory, get upstairs and get your clothes on; it's time to leave!"

Emory, "Okay, but first I have to wash my hands cuz I was scratching my tail while I was reading this book."

—

"Emory, why did you color on the wall?"

"James and Peter told me to."

—

Asa manifesto—as written by Dad:

Hi,

My name is Asa. I am also known as Destructo, Hoss, Hammer, Herman Munster, and Little Richard. I look forward to showing off my new self and talents to all of you over the holidays. I now walk, run, and climb with the agility of Lance Armstrong. I am available to visit your homes if you need some excitement. Other than two naps, I am generally awake every day from 8 a.m. to 8 p.m. I typically require a large meal upon awakening each time, along with periodic snacks. Though I am good-natured and continually smiling, I will let you know when I am hungry by screaming very loudly. (Works for me.)

My specialty is destruction. Once I finish eating, I usually just wander around the house looking for things to destroy. I can unplug every device in your home and tip over anything within arm's reach. Crashing and breaking with loud noise is preferred. I love to clean out closets, drawers, pantries, waste baskets, refrigerators, and cabinets—spilling all contents on the floor. Once I inspect everything, I always leave things on the floor. For some reason, these things and all my toys—plus Olivia's and Emory's—are occasionally put away. These, of course, must be immediately brought back out onto the floor into their proper place. Magazines, books, pots, pans, Tupperware, spices, silverware, pens, clothes, cleaning supplies, chemicals, socks, shoes, pencils, and papers all must be rearranged and redistributed daily. Each item is guaranteed to be inspected, taken apart, and broken. At no additional charge, I will also empty all purses and briefcases.

In addition to hands-on commode inspections, I also specialize in hiding items such as car keys, remote controls, wallets, and cell phones. Today, I am conducting an important experiment that involves the proper redistribution of all Q-Tips and cotton balls. These items, for some unknown reason, have, in the past, been confined to a neat basket underneath the bathroom sink. Upon completion, they will be properly distributed throughout the house. I also do garages and vehicles. Please let me know if my random redistribution services can be of use to your home.

Asa

—

Things I Have Learned—by Asa Hinkle
—as told by Dad:

"The higher I climb, the louder Mom screams."

"All the good eating stuff is kept in that big, tall white thing in the kitchen."

"Most of the really cool things are going on outside."

"Most of the really interesting stuff is kept on high shelves."

"When playing with something dangerous or anything belonging to sisters, it's best to be alone and very, very quiet."

"Mom is very predictable. It's hard to guess what Dad might do next."

"Given enough time, most things can be broken."

"Most adults outside of the family are very scary."

"Once I am full, it's cool to start tossing the remains on the floor."

"Many tasty leftovers can be found on the floor when following Emory around."

"Don't go anywhere near the bedroom after sundown; you might end up being put down."

"When they take off your clothes, it's a lot of fun to immediately run like crazy."

"Peeing is more fun when naked."

"If they would just turn me loose alone in the garage for five minutes, I could have a blast with some of that stuff."

—

This afternoon—Olivia, Emory, and I played outside in the leaves.

Olivia decided to be Pharaoh, dictating how the leaf work was to be done.

Emory was the Israelite slave, following Pharaoh's orders.

I sat in the lawn chair watching.

Kids Songs

> "Our mouths were filled with laughter, our tongues with songs of joy. Then it was said among the nations, "The Lord has done great things for them."
>
> Psalm 126:2

When my daughter Olivia, six, and her best friend, Natalie, sing—it's not with trepidation. They sing loud. They sing proud. I love to adjust the rearview mirror without them noticing so I can watch them sing in the backseat. Their faces strain with effort. They look at each other and smile. They are filled with joy. The only downside of this routine is the way their little songs have a way of getting stuck in your mind. You know what I mean. It's that song you hear for a moment that, hours later, is still rambling through your mind. Sometimes, you'll find yourself humming or singing it throughout the day. That's not really a bad thing. Unless you happen to be on an elevator at corporate headquarters with someone official-looking and you realize you are singing—"Oh, the B-I-B-L-E, yes, that's the book for me!"

With three children under the age of seven, the songs at our house are basic—and pretty much ongoing. And that's not really a bad thing, either. As we sing along as a family, I find that the simple lessons of the kid songs are pretty good reminders for me, too. Do we really need complicated theology? How about instead, "Jesus loves me, this I know. For the Bible tells me so." "Jesus loves the little children—all the children of the world." Maybe Jesus knows that I can only handle simple concepts. Maybe He just wants me to "Climb, climb up sunshine mountain and be a sunbeam for him." Maybe He knows I need to be reminded, "Be careful little feet where you go—hands what you do, heart who you trust, and mind what you think—for the Father up above is looking down in love, so be careful little feet where you go."

In a world of higher education and subject matter experts, kid songs are still a great way to learn about biblical characters like Noah, Jonah, Daniel, and a wee little man named Zaccheus. In a land of phonics and tutoring, kid songs are still the best way to memorize the names of the disciples. "Jesus called them one by one, Peter, Andrew, James, and John." We need to be reminded that "He's got the whole world in his hands and that we need to stand up—stand up for Jesus." Raising Christian soldiers is a noble parental mission, but perhaps a more fundamental call is a solo challenge from a kid song. "I may never march in the infantry, ride in the cavalry—shoot the artillery. I may never zoom o'er the enemy—but I'm in the Lord's army."

Jesus often used little children to illustrate his message. "I tell you the truth, anyone who will not receive the kingdom of God like a little child will never enter it" (Mark 10:15). "Let the little children come to me and do not hinder them, for the kingdom of God belongs to such as these" (Matthew 19:14). Jesus even indicated an inherent advantage for the "child-like" when He said, "I praise you, Father, Lord of heaven and earth, because you have hidden these things from the wise and learned and revealed them to little children (Matthew 11:25). If worship makes Jesus happy, then I suspect he is smiling broadly when Olivia and Natalie sing. Maybe, I would do well to borrow a page from their simple songbook so that I too can have the "joy, joy, joy, joy, down in my heart—down in my heart to stay."

Why Debby?

"Precious in the sight of the Lord is the death of his faithful servants."

Psalm 116:15

My cousin Debbie died on Christmas Day. Why was she dealt such a tortuous hand of adversity? Why did she have to lose her mother Maxine, her father Irvin, and her Aunt Marcella? Why must she have to grieve the loss of her sister Pam and her brother Craig? Why did she have to become the widow of her husband, Jerry? Why did she have to be ill for so much of her life? Why did she have to die at such a young age? Why did she have to say her own goodbyes to her beloved second husband Ben, her cherished daughters and sons-in-law, Gretchen, Brad, Jerra, Bobby, and her precious grandchildren? Why did she have to say goodbye to Uncle Richard and Aunt Mae? Why did she have to leave behind her wonderful cousins, Bobbie, Ben, and the Hinkles?

Debby was a fun-loving and fantastic cousin. She leaves a host of wonderful memories from Illinois, Kentucky, and beyond. She lived a magical childhood in Cairo and Dongola, as well as grand adventures at the Kentucky Hinkle Farm. Debby was funny and mischievous. She was always ready with a quick barb, and anyone was her target. I'll never forget her contagious laugh. I remember Craig torturing Debby with his pranks and shenanigans—before Debby would somehow get the last laugh. I remember how she would cringe—then laugh at the antics of Jerry and Ben.

Bobbie said, "I recall many wonderful adventures like Butter Top Coffee Cakes and the soda fountain in Dongola, Rummy, the Cairo swimming pool, going to "The Show," helping Aunt Mae with newborns, Vacation Bible School and picnics and carnival rides at Noble Park in Paducah. Debby was fun, a wonderful cousin, and a dedicated Christian." My sister, B, said, "Debby flowed through life like a river current, always strong and on the move, making the best of everything for everyone. She handled adversity with quiet strength and lots of humor. She was certainly a faithful Christian."

But why did she have to leave so soon? Debby called me her kissin' cousin. I don't really know what that means, but I do know that when she arrived, I knew a big, unwanted kiss on the cheek was coming. I'd like to have one of those kisses right now. But she's gone. Why? Maybe we're asking the wrong questions. Maybe there are better questions.

Why was she born into such a great family? Why was she given such a fun-filled childhood? Why was she such a marvelous daughter, sister, cousin, wife, mother, grandmother, and friend? Why was she so tough, resilient, and perseverant? Why did she live a life filled with such joy? Why was she blessed with two devoted husbands? Why two loving daughters and grandchildren? Why was she given wonderful cousins and church families? Why, as a youth, was she given a Bible and encouraged to read it? Why did she give her life to Christ and be baptized at an early age? Why did she perform countless selfless acts of love and service and devote her life to the cause of Christ? Why did she do such a marvelous job of raising Christian children and grandchildren? Why did she have such a great attitude despite the adversity? Why was she such an incredible example to so many? Why was she a life-long, faithful, and redeemed Christian?

I believe the answer to those better questions is simple—Jesus Christ, her Lord and Savior. He loved her. He blessed her richly. He carried her. He never left her side. He strengthened her. He comforted her. He encouraged her. He lifted her spirits when nothing else could. He was with her all along. He saved her. And now

He has lovingly welcomed her to eternal, adversity-free life in heaven. Debby always preferred the better questions. And now she has all the answers.

Big Daddy's First Day in Heaven

> "Whom have I in heaven but you? And earth has nothing I desire besides you."
>
> Psalm 73:25

My cousin Jerry awoke on his first day in heaven with strange sensations. His thoughts had immediately turned, as they always did, to family—Debby, Gretchen, Jerra, Brad, Bobby, and Big Daddy's kiddos. But Jerry realized he was suddenly incapable of experiencing any degree of problem, worry, or anxiety. In fact, Jerry could not muster even one single negative thought. His mind was full of only love, peace, joy, kindness, goodness, and faithfulness. Jerry had long ago adopted these types of thoughts but to be totally dominated by them was an amazing feeling. So, Jerry smiled his broad smile and went to see who could be knocking on his mansion door so early.

On the way to the door, Jerry passed a full-length mirror and almost passed out. He recognized the image staring back, but it was from so long ago. Was he twenty or thirty? He wasn't sure, but he did summarize his new body as "perfect." His smile grew broader as he opened the door and welcomed his first visitor, the Angel Gabriel. Gabriel was his usual radiant self, but he was also full of business. The first day of heaven is always full of important introductory events, so off they went on Jerry's most grand adventure ever. As they walked along a golden street, Jerry noticed yet another amazing development. He felt like he hadn't felt in years—no stress, no backache or pain of any kind. He tried to thank Gabriel for such an awesome feeling, but Gabriel said he was not responsible and that Jerry would soon get accustomed to his new permanent, pain-free existence. Besides, Gabriel was hurrying Jerry along to his first appointment of the day.

Jerry soon found himself in a room where he heard a booming voice announcing a complete record of his entire deeds on earth. Jerry fell to his knees. While Jerry had performed thousands of good deeds on earth, he knew he was far from perfect, and now he would face the gritty details. After a long dissertation, Jerry felt a warm glowing presence next to him and turned to see, for the first time, Jesus Himself. The glow was so strong that Jerry tried to turn away, but he couldn't because he was already embraced in a bear hug from Jesus Christ, his Lord and Savior. The bear hug between Jerry and Jesus will go down in eternal history as one of the greatest bear hugs of all times. Jesus then put his arm around Jerry and said, “Well, enough of this nonsense about sin and good deeds! I didn’t die on the cross for nothing, so let’s get started with your eternal reward!”

Jerry was instantly transported to breakfast. Jerry loved being instantly transported because time, space, and travel mean nothing in heaven, which, of course, meant no more waiting or long cramped plane rides. What a breakfast it was! Jerry’s eyes were wide as they could be as he stared at the largest, most luscious buffet he had ever seen. He could hardly contain his excitement as Gabriel whispered magic words into his ear, “It’s all free, Jerry! Everything in heaven is free. But you can still negotiate and haggle if it will make you happy.” And it made him very happy indeed, as Jerry would get the best of *every* deal in heaven. Jerry giggled and ate heartily—never gaining an ounce. After breakfast, Jerry returned to his mansion to find guests. Jerry’s mansion, by the way, was huge—humongous even—and just the opposite of all the discount motels that Jerry preferred on earth. The mansion had been perfectly built by Craig and Irvin and recently remodeled by Uncle Richard, who, because it was heaven, could complete the remodeling in less than a month, for free!

But Jerry paid little attention to the luxuries as he focused on his greeting party, his next-door neighbors, family!—Ben, Clossie, Richard, Irvin, Pam, Maxine, and Craig. They knocked Jerry to the ground with their kisses and hugs. They excitedly chatted and laughed for hours as they traded stories and loved each other. Just when Jerry thought things could be no better, Aunt Betty arrived with chicken and dumplings. Then they all got busy with plans—plans to meet all the others who had gone before and plans for mansions to be built for all those who would soon be joining the neighborhood. When the planning was over (and yes, everyone let Jerry be in charge), Jerry was instantly whisked to the largest performing arts center he had ever seen.

At first, he thought he was hearing the Freed Hardeman Madrigal Choir, but the sound was even more magical. It was the most amazing sound he had ever heard as millions were singing and praising God. Jerry, the guest of honor, sang all his favorite hymns. Even Jerry's voice was beautiful. Jerry left the worship service floating on a cloud as Gabriel escorted him to the movie room. The movie room was the latest and greatest in an ever-improving perfect heaven. Jerry was seated in a giant captain's chair facing a huge control console and the largest TV screen ever known. He was surrounded by all the people he had positively touched in his life; they numbered in the thousands. Together they enjoyed as Jerry could press the button of his choice on the console and watch any favorite memory from earth. There were many. Jerry gleefully pressed button after button and gave popsicles to all the children gathered around him. The grateful crowd—from all over the earth, including Russia, Haiti, Africa, Europe, South America, Asia, and more—enjoyed popcorn, pizza, ice cream, and movies for an evening never to forget.

Gabriel escorted a deliriously happy and peaceful Jerry home and tucked him into his new giant bed at the close of day one in heaven. *The day had been perfect*, thought Jerry, but Gabriel just smiled and told him that each day would be better than the one before. Jerry drifted off dreaming sweet dreams of Debby, his girls, and their families and the plans he was already scheming for their soon-to-be-built mansions. For Jerry, it was just the first day in heaven. Or was it a thousand years?

ON THE FARM

> "We work hard with our own hands. When we are cursed, we bless; when we are persecuted, we endure it."
>
> 1 Corinthians 4:12

When I mention the fact that I grew up on a farm, most are amazed, some in disbelief. That's not too surprising since I left the farm for college in 1977, have worked a white-collar job ever since, and I rarely have dirt under my fingernails. I often cannot remember what I had for lunch yesterday, but I have vivid memories of the first seventeen years of my life. Raccoons, tobacco, tractors, family, good food, neighbors, church, hard work, and laughter are a few thoughts that immediately come to mind. Perhaps the farm is a book itself. We'll see. For now, the words to follow are a small taste of those memories.

Son Meets Father

> "Fathers, do not exasperate your children; instead, bring them up in the training and instruction of the Lord."
>
> Ephesians 6:4

Much has been made of the wisdom passed from one farming generation to another. Those of us who have been there known that not enough has been said of the hopeless situations that farm youth such as I often encountered. You see, farming, while often depicted as a peaceful process of seasonal change and bountiful harvest, is a never-ending, problem-solving process featuring unpredictable weather, ornery animals, complicated machinery, and unique challenges managed by a stressed father with very little experience himself.

Perhaps these father-son dialogues, which you may recognize, are the real reason for the decline of the American family farm:

"Go get me a wrench!" actually means, "Don't ask questions, just run like crazy to the garage and back, and you'd better bring the right tool. Don't even think about asking me which one because I'm not really sure myself."

"You deal with those cows. It'll be a good experience for you." means, "I've had my butt kicked by those stupid animals long enough. It's your turn."

"Watch the weather for me this evening so we'll know what to do when I get home," means, "Now you can be blamed for the weather."

"Keep an eye on your little brother and sister till I get back" means, "A child will be hurt in a freakish accident in a matter of seconds. You will be found holding the evidence."

"You'd better have that done the way I want it done by the time I get back" means, "You better quickly learn to be a mind-reader."

"You do anything you want tonight. Just be ready to go early in the morning" means, "I've purposely planned a vigorous pre-breakfast agenda to curtail your late-night festivities or make you pay—your choice."

"I've showed you that a thousand times"—means—"Why can't you be a genius?

"Reach in there, way around back, and hold that thing steady while you tighten the bolt with your other hand but don't let that slip or that move"—huh?

"Get up there and hold that thing on" means, "Disregard every safety speech I've ever given you and put yourself in grave danger."

"Moan back" means, "Continue to blindly back whatever you are driving in reverse, knowing that if you hit anything, it's your fault."

"You stay here and finish up" means, "I can later blame you for anything I deem unsuccessful about this project."

"Hold this and don't move" means, "You will most likely drop from exhaustion before another word is said."

"Go into town and get me a (insert complicated description)" means, "Someone in town is about to ask you a follow-up question to which you have no answer, at which point you will guess and inevitably be wrong."

"We'll see in a few weeks how good a job you did" means, "I reserve the right to blame you for anything that may go wrong with this crop."

"Be a man. Get on in there" means, "You are about to experience pain."

"Keep that throttle just right" means, "Anything less than the desired result will be directly blamed on your inability to keep the throttle at the unspecified level."

"Take that thing apart, clean it well, and put it back together; it will be a good learning experience for you" means, "I don't have a clue how to do it. Hopefully, you'll figure it out."

"Can't you do anything right? Do I have to do everything around here? And what is wrong with you?" all mean, "You are my son, which gives me the right to use you as a convenient target for my frustration."

"This works every time..." means history is being made.

I learned to pray as a child while searching frantically for a 7/16ths box-end wrench. That's enough for now; I'm off to therapy—and hopefully college.

Back to Bandana

"Since my youth, God, you have taught me, and to this day I declare your marvelous deeds."

Psalm 71:17

Bandana, KY, is slightly east of Monkey's Eyebrow, five miles from Oscar and 45 minutes from Possum Trot. You may have heard of Bandana, as it is the fourth largest town in Ballard County. Maybe not. Actually, Bandana (population 140 in 2010) is a tiny dot on the map that was the home of the Bandana Church of Christ and some of my greatest memories of childhood. Many of the characters I remember from the 1960s are gone, but their impact will burn brightly in my mind forever. The doors of Bandana Church of Christ opened wide every Sunday morning, every Sunday evening, and every Wednesday night. I know the doors opened wide because I often unlocked the door, as the Hinkles were always first to arrive. I also knew we never missed church, and when my Little League baseball game fell on Wednesday night, my coach knew he was going to be missing a certain very unhappy third baseman.

Dad simultaneously held every position in the church except preacher. He was a valuable cog in the church of slightly less than forty members (that's counting people who rarely came). We didn't have a fleet of buses, a coffee shop, a gift shop, a ministerial staff, a mission department, a youth sports league, a website, or television broadcast, but we did have a water fountain and an orphan's home donation box nailed to the wall where people could drop their extra coins. We did not have air conditioning, but we did have open windows, ceiling fans, and heat in the winter. We also had a nursery, which my mother ran because the only babies were usually hers.

Eleven of the forty members were Hinkles. We took up an entire pew. While Dad was busy arranging his multiple hats and inventing multitasking, Mom kept a keen eye on her brood. Any shenanigans were met with an arched eyebrow. If that didn't do the trick, a trip to the men's room with Dad worked wonders. For some reason, the wooden floor of the church slanted downward toward the front. As a ten-year-old, I once deemed rolling a marble from the back to be a brilliant idea. As the marble picked up speed and eventually banged into the communion table, all eyes were on me. I can still remember the engraved words on the front of the communion table: "Do this in remembrance of Me."

I wasn't sure if I was about to become a memory, but

I was quite sure the phrase was not referring to marble rolling. Perhaps conducting my experiment during the sermon was not the brightest of ideas. Dad took me by the arm, and we went past the men's room, out the front door, and over to the nearest shade tree, where I began to fear for my life. An extended visit underneath that shade tree ensured that the marble and its wonders would never appear in church again. And they didn't.

The other six Hinkle kids made more valuable contributions. The four Hinkle sisters sang beautifully. They carried the singing once Dad got everyone rolling. "Bringing in the Sheaves" and "When the Roll is Called Up Yonder" never sounded so sweet. The Hinkle sisters eventually became a quartet. They recorded a few songs and performed at my wedding twenty-six years later. Mom sang the loudest, unfortunately. As my father often said, "She can't carry a tune in a bucket." That never stopped Mom from singing. She was the only one in our family who could not sing, but she was a big believer in singing from the heart regardless of the quality of the outcome. She always said, "It doesn't matter what it sounds like. If you really mean it, God is pleased." When we weren't laughing or cringing, we were begging her to sing "On a Hill Faraway." My mother sang her heart out for eighty-nine years. Nobody seemed to mind that she could never carry a tune.

One of the Hinkle sisters was married in that church. It was the only wedding I remember ever occurring there. It was a big deal. She married into a rather wealthy family. The groom's family traveled from some faraway place called Fort Lauderdale in a caravan of expensive cars. The trail of fancy vehicles snaked its way from Paducah to Kevil to La Center to our farmhouse and on to Bandana, then back to the farmhouse after the wedding for a reception around our kitchen table. If I remember correctly, we had pimento cheese sandwiches. I like to believe the fancy family took a liking to us and our ways—maybe even learning a thing or two—for they are still close to us some forty years later. Oh, how I would love to see a video of that event.

Worship was, of course, preceded by Sunday school. Sister Mary Bett Washam taught the only class. Everyone, not an adult, was lumped into one class. Sister Washam consistently delivered amazing teaching. Other than my parents, I credit her for anything good that has become of me. Her husband, Brother Orville Washam, was our minister. He carried a big black, well-worn Bible. He had silver hair, a soothing voice, and was trusted by all.

He offered an invitation song after each sermon. The only people I remember walking to the front of the church to be baptized over the years were the seven Hinkle children. I walked forward the day they sang "Jesus Is Tenderly Calling to Dave." One other guy walked forward once and whispered something to Brother Washam. Afterward, we all prayed for him. He must have done something very bad. The baptistery was interesting. A faded mural of the Jordan River was the backdrop for the tub located directly behind the pulpit. The water was very cold. I once asked my younger sister of her memories of baptism, and she replied, "The only thing I remember is how I kept one eye on the water and one eye on the huge spider crawling up the mural."

Brother Lee Heathcott succeeded Brother Washam. Lee and Sondra and their son Randy traveled each week all the way from Mayfield to deliver a sermon. Since the drive was so far (thirty miles), they always—and I mean always—went to our home after the morning service for lunch, a nap, and a return to evening services. Lunch was a big deal. Looking back, it was a big undertaking for my mother to make a hot lunch for fourteen prior to church every week. The lunch was placed in the oven to be ready upon our return. My favorite was meatloaf, mashed potatoes, macaroni and cheese, and fresh vegetables from our garden. I can still smell that meatloaf.

The church may have been small, but we had interesting characters. One elderly guy fell asleep every week. Obviously, he didn't have a dad there to smack him on the back of the head with a hymnal. The elder statesman of our church was Mr. Chuck. He was a grocer turned MFA insurance agent by trade. He was also the town judge. He knew everything about the Bible and taught adult Sunday School every week. On occasion, the children would stay in the sanctuary (I'm not sure what we called it, but we certainly didn't use fancy words like sanctuary). I would frequently get in trouble for asking touchy questions like, "Who exactly is going to heaven and who is not?"

Back to the shade tree. Mr. Chuck's bride was Miss Eva. She was a regal woman and the mother of the most memorable character in the church—Hodge. Something happened to Hodge when he was born. We never really knew what, but we didn't care because we loved having an adult who was our size who made us laugh. Hodge had a cool tattoo of an Indian chief on his bicep. He mowed yards for a living and wore hearing aids. He sat at the end of Chuck and Eva's pew (everyone sat in the exact same seat every week), and his hearing aids frequently made loud buzzing noises that, of course, he could not hear. Mr. Chuck would lean forward and point wildly at his ears, and all was well. We tried not to laugh because if we did, it was, you know, back to the shade tree.

The Rileys rivaled the Hinkles for attendance awards. Earnestine Riley could whip up an impressive meal herself. She and Pat were the parents of seven girls. I was informally adopted by Pat because he had a huge farm, a stocked fishing pond, and no son. My good luck began early in life. And yes, if you are keeping track, the Hinkles and Rileys accounted for over fifty percent of the church membership. I'm not sure what happened in that church, but it must have been good because, as far as I know, every living member of that church is a believer to this day.

The next generation has produced nearly a hundred believers who are still producing more. I am also impressed by the career paths of those children. There were no college graduates at Bandana Church of Christ in the 1960s, but that church has produced at least a dozen successful college graduates—plus children. I'd love to go back to Bandana in 1969. The building may be gone, but its impact and ripple effect is not. Besides, we can always go back to Bandana in our minds. I'm not sure how I got from Bandana to where I am today. Only God knows. I guess it's a long and winding road. I'm grateful the road began in Bandana.

There Lives Within My Heart A Melody

"Let them sacrifice thank offerings and tell of His works with songs of joy."

Psalm 107:22

Our parents never asked, "Will you come? Will you come?" They did, however, remind us that the Lord is in His Holy Temple, and we were about to be! The car was leaving for church in five minutes, and we had better be in it! When it was time to leave, we were resolved no longer to linger. No one stayed at home—no, not one, no, not one. We also had blessed assurance our parents were prepared in the event angry words from our tongue unbridled slipped. There was no turning back, no turning back, for they knew that Jesus loves the little children and that all other ground was sinking sand.

Church was holy, holy, holy, break thou the bread of life, give me the Bible and take everything to God in prayer. Most memorable was the singing. We were busy stepping in the light, seeking the lost, surveying the wondrous cross, and sowing in the morning, not to mention bringing in the sheaves, counting our many blessings, pressing on the upward way, and rolling the gospel chariot.

We could be walking in sunlight and receiving showers of blessing at the same time! We learned His love was deeper than the oceans and higher than the trees and that Zaccheus was a wee little man. We knew He could have called ten thousand angels, but we only knew about fifty songs. So, we'd sing them over again to me—wonderful words of life.

Dad was the song leader, and we were in the choir. Our instructions were simple—sing and be happy today! I can still hear Grandma singing, "When they ring those golden bells." I suspect she is waiting right now for us to all gather at the river. Everyone sang regardless of talent—this is so sweet to trust in Jesus, sweet are the promises and sweetest name on mortal tongue. Unfortunately, not everyone's voice was so sweet. Some, like me, were asked to sing softly and tenderly on a hill far away.

We were going down the valley, climbing Sunshine Mountain, and resting in the sweet bye and bye. We knew when to stand up, stand up for Jesus, and when to keep silent before Him. We went to the garden alone and shouted with the millions on high. We solved lots of mysteries—who was washed in the blood, who at the door was standing, what could wash away my sin, why did my Savior come to earth, why not tonight, and what to do with this little light of mine.

We knew about a royal banner, a royal diadem, how to exchange a cross for a starry crown, and what we'd rather have than silver or gold. We knew there was power in the blood, nothing but the blood, footprints of Jesus, and everlasting arms to lean on. We knew how to tune our lips, what to do on bended knee—that face to face was our destiny and that the great physician now is near.

We sang the wondrous love of Jesus on the way to church. Afterward, we would sing God be with you till we meet again and take the name of Jesus with us as we went home—in the narrow way—one step at a time. We tried to get nearer my God to thee while trying to get further away from our brothers and sisters. We even prayed for the day when I'll fly away. We marched to Zion and back to Calvary, sang onward Christian soldiers, and went yonder over the rolling river. We knew we had to surrender all, but we still did a lot of marching on, marching on because, after all, we were in the Lord's Army!

We had the joy, joy, joy, joy down in our hearts but our parents knew this was no game. We would leave soon, and they worried less, knowing anywhere with Jesus we could safely go. The wisdom went further, deep, and wide, in fact. They knew that life was not all happy songs. They knew about storms of life a raging and when upon life's billows you are tempest-tossed. We needed to know that we have an anchor where to find peace like a river and that brightly beams our Father's mercy. Did anyone ever save that fainting, struggling seaman? We didn't know what a billow was, but we knew all things were ready.

Well, time was indeed full of swift transition. The billows did roll, the storms did rage, and when they did, those old songs would come to mind at just the right time to provide comfort and direction. We had learned how firm a foundation we had, to be not dismayed what ere betide, to hide in the cleft of the Rock and that our redeemer lives. Ultimately, we knew what a friend we had in Jesus and that we must need to go home by the way of the cross.

We often sang words we didn't understand, but the message was as simple as Jesus loves me, this I know, for the Bible tells me so. It all boiled down to the old rugged cross, up from the grave he arose and victory in Jesus for those who trust and obey—all because He lives.

Often, we roamed from the sunshine of love—farther and farther away and far from the peaceful shore until we too heard the words, "O sinner, come home." Only then could we sing with meaning, amazing grace, how sweet the sound! Hallelujah, praise Jehovah! How great Thou art! When the roll is called up yonder, I'll go beyond the azure blue, just as I am. To a land beyond the river and beyond the sunset, where no storm clouds rise, to meet a God concealed from human sight in mansions bright and blessed where our precious memories will become happy reunions. Oh, what a wonderful, wonderful day—day I will never forget. What a day of rejoicing that will be! For now, we'll be standing on the promises until we've gone the last mile of the way.

Now please mark in your hymnals these final verses of name that tune. Praise Him, praise Him ever in joyful song. Be more than almost persuaded to thank those who loved you enough to insist on such an upbringing. Emulate them as you raise your own, write on their hearts every word. Finally, when you are unsure of your step, listen closely, and those wonderful old songs telling the old, old story will lead you safely all the way.

Written for Mom: She couldn't sing very well but never let that stop her from singing from the heart and being masterful at training little Christians through songs.

And written for Dad: who really was the song leader—and still is—by his example.

Finally, I salute the rest of the Hinkle choir:
Al, Brenda, Cara, Ella, Mo, Annie, and Grandma.

Tobacco Patch Lessons

> "For gaining wisdom and instruction; for understanding words of insight."
>
> Proverbs 1:2

Except for smoking, everything about tobacco is difficult. Cutting tobacco (that means harvesting to those of you who haven't had the pleasure) must be one of the most physically exhausting tasks in the history of manual labor. Working in a coal mine and building pyramids couldn't be fun, but I'd jump into a storytelling contest with a miner or an Egyptian any day. I won't bother explaining the details to those who haven't been there because you wouldn't believe it anyway. Just take my advice and run fast in the other direction if you're ever invited to one of these parties.

In the 1970s, boys earned their college and spending money by paying their dues in the tobacco patch. Anything bought with tobacco money was something of value. I hear that most of this inglorious work is now handled by imported labor. That's a shame, in a way, because the tobacco patch teaches lessons like no other classroom. I've never made an adult nickel with my skills honed by carrying a hatchet and spike, but I did take some valuable lessons with me.

The first lesson I learned is that everything is relative. Ten-year-old boys weren't to play with sharp knives, but the safety police were nowhere to be found when they handed out razor-sharp tobacco cutting knives and pointed steel spikes. In fact, the first thirty minutes of work were spent sharpening the weapons. If I saw someone in public today with either of these tools, I would alert the police immediately.

The second lesson I learned is that if anything is as painful as tobacco, then get as far away from it as humanly possible. Working in tobacco taught me to get off the farm, go to college, get a job in an air-conditioned building, and never go back.

Those lessons lead to some interesting final observations. While my tobacco memories are a blur of humor and pain, the men are forever etched in my mind, and they are some of the finest people I've ever known. In fact, when compared to some of the lunatics I've reported to since donning a suit and tie, these guys should be teaching at the Wharton School of Business. For example, no self-respecting tobacco farmer would ever reverse a logical course of action because of a memo from the home office. A tobacco farmer would never change their mind in mid-season and start raising corn. A tobacco farmer would never change strategy from one day to the next based on mood. Tobacco farmers would never hold meetings in the middle of the day when work was being done, nor would they have wrap-up meetings, download meetings, or conference calls. Tobacco farmers do not conduct annual reviews for their employees, and they have a totally different concept of team-building exercises.

More importantly, tobacco farmers are just plain honest. They pay a fair market wage. They don't change your pay after they've given their word. They don't demand you do the impossible just because they need to make more money. They don't react to the competition, they don't play politics, they don't fret over promotions, and I never recall a tobacco farmer enticing me with dreamy promises of valuable stock on their farm.

When a tobacco farmer meets you at the end of the row for some instruction, you know exactly what to do when they leave. That's more than I can say for many conversations I've had at work lately. Tobacco farmers don't entertain customers with lavish dinners. In fact, I've learned that I'd rather be told the truth over a ham sandwich than be lied to over lobster. I'd rather hear the straight truth under a shade tree than have my leg pulled at the Plaza Hotel, and I'd rather ride a tobacco wagon for an honest day's pay than fly in first-class for a phony cause.

The only common thread I see between these two worlds is one of self-protection. I learned early on never to turn my back on a tobacco co-worker holding sharp objects. I've learned to be critically important in the business world as well, despite the lack of sharp objects. Don't get me wrong; I'm not going back to the tobacco patch. I'm much too smart for that. I just yearn for simple, straightforward honesty.

Maybe I could bring a little common sense to the boardroom. I wonder what would happen if my old buddy, Woodrow Piper, ran my company for just one week. I know we would make a ton of money. He would either turn things around with good old-fashioned horse sense or, at the very least, we'd have enough humor from one day to win an Oscar for best comedy screenwriting.

So, here's to Forrest Burns, Billy Joe, William Earl, and Tobe, all veterans of the real tobacco wars. I could tell you many funny stories about them. All gone but William Earl; they were walking, talking, Norman Rockwell characters

who raised more tobacco than North Carolina. Finer men
you'd never meet. Smart, too. Why do you think they
hired guys like me instead of doing it themselves?

The Greatest Ride of My Life

"Surely you have granted him unending blessings and made him glad, with the joy of your presence."

Psalm 21:6

I had to position myself very carefully so that I could be just like him, occasionally peeking from the corner of my eye to make sure my pose was perfect. My elbow rested in the open truck window with the wind blowing into my smiling face. Saturday was the day we went to town. I shared him with my brothers and sisters, but on an occasional trip, I was an only child, and I loved it. We waved whether we knew people or not. Dad said it was good to be friendly. Our truck was a powerful, brand new, refurbished, shiny, used, slightly rusted but perfect Chevrolet.

The drive from home to town was three miles. Sometimes we talked, and sometimes we didn't; it was about being together, not making things happen. First stop was McElya's Phillips 66 for gas and town news. Mr. Aaron was friendly, and he'd check your oil. He let me pump gas and helped me climb a ladder to clean the windshield. He wore short-sleeve coveralls without any shirt. The station is still run by a guy named Rex. In those days, though, he was known for something quite different.

Every Tuesday and Friday night, our rural high school gymnasium, the Green Palace, was packed, and it must have seated about 100,000. With the smell of popcorn filling the air, the band would rock on as the Bombers took the floor for basketball action. Long before Chapman, this Rex was the King. He wore number 44 and dominated the floor. But the team was much more. Howle, Humphrey, Hunt, Deweese, Hammonds, and Henderson—this team wearing green was more important than the Boston Celtics. I have no idea why, but I can still tell you the numbers that each player wore. We sat in the bleachers for all the home games or glued to the transistor radio for road games at faraway places like Hickman and Fulton. WPAD radio delivered all the action on the worldwide Ballard Bomber network.

In town, we made all the rounds. Important stops were made at the Farmers Co-op and Graves Brothers Plumbing—they stood side by side. The Co-op had everything a farmer could need, even advice. They loaded everything for free in the back of your truck. If we didn't need anything, we stopped anyway to hear Kayo's jokes or farmers like Woodrow telling big stories around an old fireplace. Everyone wore a hat; John Deere and Ford were the favorites.

If an animal was sick, we stopped at Doc Coffee. He could fix a horse or a cow or even your cat. The sick people all went to see Doc Dyer, or ten miles away to see Doc Hunt. ("Just put what you can afford in the cigar box on the way out the door.") Eight Balls barbershop was a must once a month. Nothing was fancy here, just an old twirling barber pole that wasn't old-fashioned then, a burr haircut, a couple of jokes, and a lollipop for sitting still. We never stopped at Mr. Carl's. It was a hub for men, but a pool hall was strictly forbidden for good Christians like us—or at least for another year or two until I could drive my own car, park it around the corner and sneak in the side door.

Mom bought her stamps at the post office from Bernice, who probably saw a little of everything except anthrax in her career. Mom shopped at Whipple's Food Market, where I would get my first job. Whipple's is still a landmark today. It was around long before the Charmin commercial and was founded by the Whipple Brothers and their wives. The second generation was my group of friends—brothers Joe Brooks and Allen and their mother—Ada Allen. "Just sign for your groceries, and we'll send you a bill—if you need a little credit, we won't let you go hungry." Glen was the butcher, and Ben followed him, but Marie Beth was the straw that stirred the drink. She's served six decades at Whipple's. I figure she's sold more groceries than Kroger.

I now shop at stores with hundreds of aisles, but none fare well against the Whipple benchmark. No one cares more for you and your food. We always went to the bank to see our financial friends, Eddie Gene and Curt. We never waited in line, and we never did paperwork—just a promise, a handshake, and a signature. I know that for a fact because I later did it myself, all because of my last name. Their candy wasn't bad either. Roy was the Sheriff (later gave me lectures, not tickets) and Moss L.P. Gas trucks were a routine sight. George ran a pharmacy complete with a soda counter. Mr. Jones took the call when you met your Maker. Mr. Chuck could sell you some MFA insurance while telling you a story about seeing Babe Ruth play baseball.

Everyone believed about the same thing religiously, but we had eight churches for mostly unexplained reasons. Driving by La Center Elementary on Saturday was a joy. The school was closed, and so were the books—no math, no homework, and no Mrs. Wiggins, the toughest fifth-grade teacher in the galaxy. Three different pedestrians were fixtures in town. Judge Walters wore white and a big straw hat. Howard was the little guy who walked but rarely talked. Small but strong as an ox was our old friend Hodge who went to our church.

Hodge was simple and was everyone's buddy. He cut grass for a living, but not like guys today. He pushed his own mower and carried his own gas can. He was a working machine, daylight till dark, even mowing the entire town park with his push mower—once a week. Bob, Donnie, and Clarence stocked about every kind of appliance, TV, or fireplace you could need. It was my favorite stop since I could see my good friend and a great American, Donnie's son—Jeff. Jeff and Dennis Craig were my baseball-playing friends from town. Jeff was cool because he lived in town and played guitar. I still think his death at the age of 16 was one of the greatest injustices in the history of the world.

Last stop on the trail was Brockman's service center because you could trust your car to the man who wore the star—"Mr. Fix It." Men fixed their own cars in those days, at least until they got stumped. That's where Bill came in. Since leaving home, I've heard he's retired five times only to open another shop somewhere in town. La Center's not Mayberry; it's much better because it all really happened. The people weren't perfect, but neither were we. You could do a lot worse than to grow up there. Some of the characters are gone, some are still there, but they all live forever in my mind. You may think I exaggerate or juggle my facts. I beg to differ. It's my story, and it's perfect for me. My hometown will always be special. Maybe it was the people, or maybe it was me. I tend to credit the guy driving the truck.

Hag

"One who has unreliable friends soon comes to ruin, but there is a friend who sticks closer than a brother."

Proverbs 18:24

A lanky kid from somewhere sauntered, all arms and legs, into my teenage life, and things have never been quite the same. I didn't mind the academic butt-kicking he immediately administered, for he kept me laughing the entire time. His name is Ken, but he was a Hag from day one. So, what is a Hag? After thirty-six years of camaraderie, I feel semi-qualified and wholeheartedly compelled to share my viewpoint. A Hag is a Haggard but mostly a Piper. He is part Bobby Ray, part Carolyn, a dash of Irene, and a strong shot of Woodrow. He's a farmer, a fighter, and a lover. He was a track star on his way to high hurdle adventure. He knows his way around a grain bin, but he's more at home in a fast car. He could chop tobacco, haul hay, down a six-pack, and ace the LSAT all before dark. He can outwork you for weeks on end while closing the party every night. Hag is energetic, intelligent, passionate, successful, and forever flirting with a loveable dose of paranoia.

Hag has a thorough understanding of loyalty, the law, human nature, motorcycle gangs, and the occasional recreational diversion. He charged head-first into life and has yet to let up. He is LeiAndra, Robbie, Jolie, and a lot of Joe Craig. He's earned the respect of family, friends, professors, clients, policemen, judges, and opponents. From Farless and Hart to the guy on the street, he will forever be the champion of the underdog in need. Hag is delightful contradiction. He can rail about a "battle ax" and defend her in the same sentence. He is a tractor and a BMW. He is a filet mignon and a ham sandwich. He is Bob Seger, Ozzie Osborne, and the Kentucky Wildcats. He is Aruba and Hinkleville. He is a friend to the wealthy and a friend to the poor. He can be as intense as nuclear threats or as laid back as a Key West sunset. He was an in-your-face brawler, but he also teaches a mean Sunday School class. He lives an even better one.

Hag is a simple yet complex character. He has the uncanny ability to be irrational and compelling simultaneously. He's usually correct on any subject. And please remember, you may forget, but he will not. Hag is far more kind, humble, and generous than he wants you to know. Woe to the proud and arrogant who carelessly stumble into his path. Blessed are the underprivileged that catch his eye. To be his friend is pure joy—his enemy, not so much. Not a Republican and not quite a Democrat, he is a unique Robin Hood of sorts who certainly believes in wealth re-distribution, with much of it finding its way to his pocket—as it rightfully should—and then usually on to others.

Despite his outstanding legal legacy, he is no politician—too much brutal honesty and common sense. You want hilariously funny? Who can hear him belly laugh and not join in? But his stories are not to be recorded in written history. They are to be told, elaborated, explained, exaggerated, and properly savored in good company. Skip the fiction—his real life is much better. You may never fully understand a Hag, but you will enjoy. So, what do you get when combine a brilliant mind, headstrong parents, a wise old granddaddy farmer, a quality education, and a great wife? Well, you get a Hag, and you certainly get someone who is loyal and devoted.

If I chose one person to fight through enemy lines and rescue me from danger—it would be Hag. I suspect he would show up early with a smile, cold beverage, and wisecrack. His life is one of stunning peaks and dark valleys. Through it all, he keeps climbing, as does his lovely bride LeiAndra who surely has seen it all. Someday she will receive her eternal crown for standing by her man and being exactly what he needed her to be. God stayed up late creating Hag. I suspect He is very proud of the race Hag is running. Hag's a treasure for those of us along for the ride—those of us for whom he would run through walls. I hope he knows that we would, without hesitation, do the same for him.

The Country Mechanic

> "A time to weep and a time to laugh, a time to mourn and a time to dance."
>
> Ecclesiastes 3:4

I walked into the dump of an office and was met by floor-to-ceiling stacks of newspapers, invoices, manuals, and anything else that may have been thrown in the general direction of the piles over the past several years. It's one of those places where there is but a single path winding throughout the room. I asked the old man if his son, David, was handy. He replied, "He ain't handy, but he's here. I'll git him fer ya." I stared at the office Christmas tree (it's August) and kept quiet so as to not disturb David's intense concentration on the computer screen and his violent one-finger typing. I admired his oversized Elvis glasses, his huge belly, gym shorts, white legs, hi-top tennis shoes, and his leopard t-shirt with the sleeves and neck ripped out. (I'd send you a photo, but you wouldn't believe it). I took in all the posted signs of inappropriate humor. I marveled at the hi-tech phone headset he was wearing with base clipped to what was left of the neck of his t-shirt. I dared not laugh at the grease stain on his nose. I tried to make small talk with his chain-smoking father, who didn't seem to be impressed when I complimented his reputation of integrity. David chimed in with, "Every now and then, a car'll make a liar outta me, but other than that, we try to keep er on the up and up."

I asked the old man how long he had been here. He replied, "Two years. Course we been in business since 1954 if that's what ya mean." (I assume the old place was condemned.) David smiled at me with a toothless grin and a comical sense of achievement as he mercifully completed the computer entries. "Ha! 299.08—told ya I'd keep her under 300." I thought I was near escape but didn't realize that it was now time for the all-important visual demonstration of the broken part, how it was supposed to operate, why it didn't, where she give out, and what he did about it. I believe my patience and feigned interest may have gained me some good will for my next visit. He laid the broken part on a stack of something. I'm confident it will still be in the same spot next time I visit.

I thought for a moment about the possibility that David might have a wife and children. Then I quickly dismissed that visual. David laughed harder and louder and longer (over nothing) in that thirty minutes than

I usually do all week. I think he is a real happy guy. He probably has more money than me. Then again, maybe he was happy because he went to the State Fair in my jeep and chased women. I'm thankful that I didn't inherit the car fixing gene that was such a part of my Dad and Grandpa, but the experience was so memorable that I was tempted to stop at Fern Moody's next door for a cold beer. But I didn't.

A Road Well-Traveled

> "I think it is right to refresh your memory as long as I live in the tent of this body,"
>
> 2 Peter 1:13

An exciting yet frightening destination loomed on my horizon. My perception of Ballard Memorial High School was no less grandeur than the average adult's image of Carnegie Hall, Madison Square Garden, and Grand Central Station combined. BMHS was an incredibly humongous campus featuring monster-sized buildings and the largest gymnasium in America—as far as I knew. The place housed hundreds of teachers and thousands of students. Every single one of those students was older than I, and most of them were bigger. This twelve-year-old was facing quite a challenge.

Some of my memories are brilliantly etched and easily retrieved—most of them first and many of them, for some reason, occurring in my second decade of life. First friend (and a good one), Burns, first job, Whipples' Food Market, first baseball glove, Rawlings, first car, Monte Carlo, and first kiss—not going there. A million memories have come and gone in forty years and most forgotten, but not these and certainly not my first of BMHS.

When Rachel's big yellow bus stopped at the front door of BMHS, I experienced my first and only urge to ever stay on a school bus. This was a big step for a farm boy accustomed to wide-open spaces and long summer days. Peer pressure and Rachel's stern urgings made the choice easy. Everyone inside this bustling place seemed to be on important missions and know exactly where they were going—except me. Walking the halls of BMHS for the first time felt like walking a gauntlet through a giant canyon. The mile-high lockers on either side were obscured by tall, smirking guys staring at my every vulnerable move. I might as well have had a neon light above my head that flashed "rookie."

Fortunately, reality arrived at Ballard soon after I did. The upperclassmen were, for the most part, not dangerous ogres, nor were the teachers. Like an animal in a forest, danger was always present, but at least I learned where the safe zones were. I also learned that the best part of high school was the annual graduation when another crop of smirking faces disappeared forever, and I moved one rung higher on the ladder. The safe zones I identified were home to some amazing characters. Long before Jerry Seinfeld, Hagood was the king of observational humor.

I see him these days only at reunions, but he still leaves me laughing. Another comedic genius was Hammonds. No one was immune to his sharp wit and keen one-liners. Add Terrell, Kubica, and Haney to these two, and you've got a terrific sitcom.

As the months went by, the safe zones grew, and so did our confidence, sometimes at alarming levels. That's probably why they make seniors graduate. We had independence, a driver's license, pretty girls, a few dollars, and raging hormones. We were a dangerous lot. Within the safe zones were some keen minds. Powell, Graves, Tietyen, and Martin had the audacity to never score less than an A. I was in tall academic cotton. Powell's perfect answers were topped only by his artistic ability. His pencil sketches I observed in high school are now award-winning art. Graves, Tietyen, and Martin are probably professors at Harvard now. Believe it or not, they achieved their academic feats without the benefit of computers, cellphones, or even calculators. Imagine that, academic excellence with only pencil and paper!

In case you're interested, we also survived without internet, e-mail, cable TV, ESPN, VISA, HBO, GPS, UPS, BCS, CNN, FOX, VCR, CSI, DVD, SUV, or IBM. We had no software or hardware—just Coach Wear. If there is a BMHS Hall of Fame, Coach Wear is in it. No scheming little adolescent ever escaped his narrow eyes. No smart-aleck gym student ever got the last word. No miscue was beyond his wrath. He taught the Carson Newman Shuffle and the Three-Guard Weave. He could work a referee and cut you off in mid-sentence with his sharp wit. When he talked out of the side of his mouth, you listened. His hair, his clothes, his confidence, his humor, and his stories were all legendary.

My jump shot was no match for Scott, Russell, or Goode, so I first tasted humility sitting at the end of the basketball bench with Allred and Davenport, wearing an ill-fitted uniform with some outrageous number, like sixty-three, and waiting to be waved in with thirty seconds left in the game. I started only one game, where I was rudely introduced to the one-three-one full-court trap press of Paducah Tilghman. My career as a starting point guard lasted less than 1 minute. Jogging to the bench was the only time I got safely across the mid-court line. I spent a lot of time on that bench. It was worth every moment just being there to see Allred purposefully foul out all five in one of those thirty-second cameo roles. He said he could do it, and he did.

BMHS had no shortage of teaching wizards.

Overconfident boys needed an Elliott to keep them in line. Lane was a friend and a teacher. Simmons and Wynn knew more math than NASA. Barnett was original and popular. Carpenter and Keyser were undoubtedly noble, attempting to walk our crew through biology and chemistry. Shelton and Roberts made school fun. They took no guff, but they had their laughs. I bet millions with Roberts on Monday night football. Every week, one of us wrote a phony check. I think I still owe him a million or two.

Another live wire, Hutcherson, was wise enough to begin teaching our last year. Allen, Davis, and Houston were first class. Crice was tough but entertaining. The Trice era was just beginning. Owen was a character not soon forgotten. Dunn's enthusiasm deserved better than us. It's amazing to think that at that time, those mentoring figures were younger than I am now. The only lesson I remember from BMHS is a Skidmore comment, "There's two of you, young man, one very good and one very bad; it will be interesting to see which one wins." I guess the battle rages on.

The leadership at Ballard had little patience for cynical minds like mine. Anderson was the wise old owl, McGregor his trusted lieutenant, while secretary Myers was the glue that held the school together.

Superintendent Buchanan had the presence of a Supreme Court Justice. I'd probably be nervous if I saw him today. The toughest job at Ballard was supervising the shop. Only a veteran like Wells could avert total disaster. What genius decided that high school boys needed access to power tools? The clowns in my class could swipe your book, toss it to the back, rip it through the band saw, and have both pieces back on your desk before a substitute teacher could finish cleaning his glasses.

A real funny guy, then and now, is Wright, who has a wealth of comedy material from coaching Ballard's first football team (of which I was a member after wisely switching from basketball). The team may be champions now, but a price was paid to get there. Hurst and Buchanan made for a powerful backfield. Who can forget Davis tipping the play to the defensive line in a lop-sided game? The result was his running back friend, Terrell being immediately crushed. We had a star named Wildman Webb and a lineman who stored cigarettes and a lighter in his playing uniform. Why is it that I can't remember what I had for lunch yesterday, but I clearly remember these details?

We had dedicated coaches like Sydboten and Morris. We had devoted cheerleaders like Meredith, Waldon, and

Stewart. We had loyal tough guys like Clouser, Geveden, Shepherd, and Big Bill. I set a school record with a seventy-eight-yard touchdown pass. Who cares if Key ran seventy-seven of those yards after catching the pass? Football was fun.

Ballard came in pairs—Workman and Perry, Smith and Jett, Jeanna and Stacey, Murphy and Steele, Temple and Hicks, LaVerne and Shirley, Tim and Charley. Reynolds is a memorable character, and Bondurant was always up to something. Is the Kevil gang of Bone, White & Dowdy still around? Whatever happened to Herrington, Craig, Farmer, or Zanetta? Where's Bernadette, Christie or Bass? How about King? Could you find nicer people than Sybil, Morphew, or Mariner?

Ballard was music. Bob Seger had night moves, and Boston was more than a feeling. Rod Stewart had Maggie and Peter Frampton, a talking guitar. Fleetwood Mac, Kiss, Queen, Styx, Foghat, Eagles, and Foreigner's "Feels Like the First Time"—and it was. Some songs can still transport you in an instant. Ballard was FFA, the Fin 'N Feather, Tin-Can-Alley, going parking, Cairo, Powder Puff Football, the Turf Club, and the Green Palace. Ballard was the Diary of Anne Frank, a homecoming dance, Metropolis, a tobacco patch, Smokey and the Bandit, and Eight-Track tapes.

Ballard was Smith's van, Parker's Cutlass, Mills, the Barlow Bottoms, and the La Center Park. We wore green shoes, green jackets, and green uniforms that made the band look like Revolutionary War leprechauns. We pulled every possible prank, invented cruel methods of aggravation, and told our parents about half of everything that happened.

It's a shame how we often rated, judged, and classified each other, but at least it prepared us for the world ahead. No terrorists, no mortgages, no children, no tattoos, no earrings, no debt, no gray hair, no fear, and no PlayStation 2. Elvis was still alive. No disappointment, no failure, no heartache, or divorce. No AIDS or school shootings, but we did have the Ten Commandments, school prayer, and a good whippin' for breaking the rules. Where did all the paddles go? No Mike Tyson, Mike Piazza, or Mike Ditka, but we did have Jonesy, much better than the other Mikes, if you ask me. It was a time before Tiger, Oprah, Di, Prince, and Tom Cruise. Before Sting, Madonna, Shaq, Kobe, Brittainy, and J-Lo. Before Saddam, Ben Laden and Ben Affleck. We had classes in math, English, and history, but no classes in life—the class we needed most. No problem—we wouldn't have believed it, anyway.

We've lost parents, hair, friends, innocence, and marriages, but we've gained children, wisdom, and perspective. Above all, Ballard is people. Life-long friends and great Americans like Burns, Haggard, Hutcherson, Hurst, and Hicks, now a powerful minister. Ballard is fine, hard-working people from solid, God-fearing families. Ballard is people who have gone on, Webb, Allred, young Hag, the young Hutch, Rusty, Parker and Shaunza. Ballard is a million people gone in a million directions on a million different missions. Ballard is champions still there, raising more champions. Ballard is teachers, students, parents, and memories. Ballard is a place, a place in your mind, a pretty good place.

Whipple's

> "Remember the days of old; consider
> the generations long past. Ask your father
> and he will tell you, your elders, and they will
> explain to you."
>
> Deuteronomy 32:7

Joe Brooks Whipple locked the front door and, with tears in his eyes, handed the key to the new owner. After eighty-one years, Whipple's was no more.

Whipple's was a legendary landmark for over eight decades in rural La Center, Kentucky. The grocery store of three generations was opened in 1931, in the midst, of the great depression. Joe Brooks Whipple's grandfather, A.C. Whipple, invested his last eighteen hundred dollars to open A.C. Whipple and Sons—a general store on main street in La Center. His store featured dry goods and groceries. In that era, customers were very careful with their precious dollars. Many shopped three times a day, for only one meal at a time. A.C. was known for precisely taking care of his customers. He knew everyone in town by name, and he would always stock their exact needs. He often stocked, in advance, select items, like shoes, in the perfect size, knowing when a certain customer's shoes would be worn out. A.C.'s favorite line was, "I got just what you need!"

His general store featured a long wooden counter where customers would lay their selections, a coal stove, and much later, Whipple's had one of the first air-conditioners in town. During working hours, baby Joe Brooks (usually referred to by his first and middle name) slept in an open dresser drawer in the store. A.C hired his sons, Andrew, James (Joe Brooks' father), and Adron. All three sons served in World War II. Adron served in the Navy, while James and Andrew served in the Army Air Corps.

Adron continued a career in the military, and James and Andrew returned home to help their father. Andrew and James convinced A.C., in 1950, to phase out dry goods and focus exclusively on groceries. They changed the name to Whipple's. A.C. died in 1952, leaving the store to his sons.

Joe delivered groceries in his youth, standing on the sideboard of his father's truck. He always timed his deliveries well—to get a lunch treat from the ladies he served. Joe Brooks was twenty-one and in college in 1969 when his father, James, died at the age of fifty-three. Within a year of James' death, Andrew sold his half of the store to Joe Brooks and his mother, Ada Allen Whipple

(Miss Ada) then Andrew retired. Joe Brooks' brother, Allen, served in the Navy. He, too, returned to work at the store. Allen died at age thirty-six, and Miss Ada lived to be ninety-six years old.

Joe Brooks had this to say, "Allen was a great guy, very smart, and we got along well. Miss Ada was a wonderful woman. After retiring from teaching school, she was our bookkeeper for many years. Many thought her to be stern, but she was just serious about her business. I remember her as a great mother and the one who always knitted sweaters for the homeless. We all took our business seriously, but I always told folks I never worried about anything because Allen and Miss Ada did all the worrying."

In 1974, Miss Ada, Joe Brooks, and Allen expanded the store to its current size. A new era of Whipple's was born. Of the hundreds of employees who served at Whipple's, perhaps the most valuable was Glen Wildharber. Glen worked thirty-nine years at Whipple's as a meat cutter and General Manager. He had this to say, "Time went by fast because every day was different. The customers were great. Joe Brooks and I never had a difference, never a cross word. I really enjoyed my time at Whipple's."

Another key employee was Marie Beth Everett. Joe Brooks recalls, "Marie Beth had a tough family life, but she never brought it to work. No one could check out customers faster and more accurately than Marie Beth. She was loyal and had a great sense of humor, but she was all business. She was very good at what she did."

Whipple's, though, did much more than exist and survive. They were always profitable and successful, even in the last days, competing against superstores in the nearest city. But business did not define Whipple's. In many ways, they were the heart and soul of La Center and rural Ballard County. Customers were loyal, and they loved Whipple's because Whipple's loved them. Joe Brooks and Glen knew their customers by name, and they cared for them.

Of course, Leah, Joe Brooks' wife of forty-nine years, played a major role in the history of Whipple's. She remembers, "In the terrible ice storm of 2009, we had no power or generator, but we stayed open. Customers were invited to shop for much-needed family groceries while wearing a headlight. Joe Brooks checked out each customer using an old-fashioned manual cash register. It was our way of serving the community that served us well. We believed in and practiced the Golden Rule. Joe Brooks ran an honest business. We did our best to always deal honestly with customers, employees, and suppliers."

Joe Brooks leaves reminders he instilled in his employees over fifty years. "Always greet your customers by name, by Mr. or Mrs., until they tell you otherwise. Always count their change for them and place it in their hand. Always smile and say thank you. Always sack their groceries, carry the groceries to the car and tell them thank you again."

And in addition to long hours at the store, Joe Brooks found time to serve his community. For thirty-two years, he has been a leader in the La Center Town Council. He has served on the Board of Directors for the local bank and the telephone company. Whipple's has been financial contributor to the local schools and their church for many years. And if that service was not enough, Joe Brooks always allowed customers to charge on credit if they could not afford to pay. He long ago lost track of the money he loaned or was never repaid. And above all, Joe Brooks and Leah have been loving and devoted parents to their two daughters, Rebecca and Caroline, and their two grandchildren, Ryn and Patrick.

On Whipple's last day, Whipple's invited the first customer of the newest store, Mrs. Paulette Petty, to be their last customer. Joe Brooks rang up the final sale, and Caroline sacked the groceries. The door was locked, the key handed over, and Joe Brooks greeted the crowd of customers and former employees. Hugs for everyone, tears for all. The success story of Whipple's began a new chapter.

Joe Brooks concluded, "We tried to do what was right. We always told the truth. We worked long hours and never thought a thing about it because that's what my father and grandfather did. It worked." From 1931 to 2012, from A.C. to Joe Brooks, Whipple's was a hallmark of success and quality service—to their country, to family, customers, employees, Ballard County, and the town of La Center. The world needs more Whipple's.

Author's note. I miss Whipple's, especially when I shop at most stores in the city where I now live. No one ever cared more for you and your groceries than Whipple's. I took special privilege in this story by offering a bit of color commentary because I was there. I sacked groceries at Whipple's from 1974 to 1977. I learned many valuable life lessons at Whipple's, and for that, I am very grateful.

DEVOTIONS I HAVE MET

Devotions *read* are wonderful,
devotions *seen* are priceless and rarely forgotten.

"I'd rather see a sermon than hear a sermon."

Edgar Guest

Follow Me

> "Come, follow me," Jesus said, "and I will send you out to fish for people."
>
> Matthew 4:19

When my son was four years old, his favorite game was "rock in a hole." Every afternoon when we returned from his pre-school, he would jump out of the car and begin excitingly repeating, "Rock in the hole, Daddy! Rock in the hole, Daddy!" So off we went, walking down the sidewalk and gathering rocks along the way. After a block or so, we came to our favorite destination—a sewer grate on the edge of the street. My son then, with great enjoyment, would drop the rocks, one by one, into the grate. Once the mission was complete, he was perfectly satisfied and ready to go home.

One day, our daily adventure took a spiritual twist. Upon depositing the last rock in the hole, my son began walking home—in the wrong direction. No amount of convincing could change his mind. He was absolutely and positively sure he was going in the right direction.

Finally, I tossed the sobbing tyke over my shoulder and carried him home—in the right direction. As I walked the short block home with a kicking, screaming, and crying four-year-old on my shoulder, I heard a very distinct voice in my mind, "When I take you in a different direction that you think is wrong, don't kick, scream or fight." I thought little of it, but time changed everything. In less than three years, our family was split asunder, and my world was turned completely upside down. I had been taken in a totally different direction.

The Evangelist Philip had a similar experience in terms of directional advice. (Acts 8:26–40). Successfully preaching to large crowds in Samaria, an angel appeared and sent Philip to the desert. The desert? There, Philip encountered an Ethiopian to whom he explained the gospel. Philip led him to Jesus Christ and then baptized him. Many believe that Ethiopians became the first convert in the continent of Africa, thus ultimately changing the spiritual fortunes of millions.

Once, while teaching a Bible class entitled "Your Next Assignment," we examined the characteristics of Philip's adventure. Philip had been drawn away from a comfortable setting, sent to an uncomfortable and unlikely place, and then given an unusual assignment. Our class challenge became, "What is your next assignment? Will you accept?"

Upon class dismissal, a woman approached me with tears in her eyes. She handed me a small, folded piece of paper (which I have to this day). Written on the note was, "My next assignment is to go to prison and forgive the man who murdered my daughter. I accept." So, in most unusual ways, Philip, the woman in the Bible class, and I all experienced the same. And, after unbelievable circumstances and some passage of time, immense blessings flowed for us and for many others.

So, what is my next assignment? Even if that assignment is unusual, unexpected, and uncomfortable, am I ready and willing to accept it?

Prayer Warriors

"Pray continually."

1 Thessalonians 5:17

During one of the most difficult seasons of my life, a friend introduced me to a sweet, elderly woman named Dorothy. At her inquiry, I told her my story. She looked me in the eye and simply said, "I will pray for you." I appreciated the gesture but thought little of it afterward.

Several weeks later, I encountered Dorothy at church. Given her age and likely poor memory, I helped our greeting by saying, "Hi, Dorothy, I'm Dave." She looked me right in the eye again and said, "I know very well who you are, Dave Hinkle. I've been praying for you since we met." "Prayer Warrior" may be an overused term, but I suspect Dorothy is indeed one.

I doubt I am the only one she has prayed for. She likely has prayed countless times for countless numbers of people. We'll never know because Dorothy is too humble to say. The Bible, in fact, instructs us to go to a private place for our prayer. Not everyone is a famous preacher or one out in the front leading a ministry band. Some are quietly and anonymously working behind the scenes. I believe Dorothy is the latter.

Prayer is mentioned specifically forty-one times in the Bible and remains one of the cornerstones of the Christian faith. Jesus prayed more than anyone in the Bible. He prayed for His mission. He prayed for His disciples. He prayed for all believers. He prayed for friends and family. He prayed for groups and for individuals. He prayed for multitudes. He prayed alone. He encouraged prayer. He modeled prayer. He prayed without ceasing.

In my conversations with other believers, I have learned a lot about prayer. Some pray for hours, some very little. Some pray silently, some out loud. Some on their knees, some while in the shower. Some pray in a closet. Some pray with others. Some pray with the famous, some with lonely folks in hospitals. Some pray long, elegant prayers, some short and simple. Many are very hesitant to talk about their prayer life. Some pray for themselves, some pray only for others, and undoubtedly experience what Oswald Chambers calls "the ongoing grind of intercessory prayer."

I understand because often I am overwhelmed by Bible study and prayer requests and the prayer needs of family, friends, neighbors, co-workers, and the world around me.

And, of course, that all comes after prayerful confession, praise, personal asks, and gratitude. That's a lot of prayer for all of us! My purpose here is not to judge or evaluate. I'm only an observer. I do, in fact, suspect, though, that Jesus is more interested in my heart than He is in my prayer style. I also know that I once snickered at those who prayed thanks for "little things," like the beauty of flowers, a convenient parking spot, or a warm place to sleep. After a few years of living and some personal adversity, I no longer snicker. After all, God's probably not too interested in my big picture or my long-term strategic plan.

So, where am I going with all this? I'm not sure. In many ways, I find the whole process of prayer somewhat mystifying. But what I do know is that He told me to pray and that prayer works. So, I will do it. I also have enough sense to pray thanks.

Thank you, Jesus. Thank you, Dorothy.

The Coin

> "Jesus performed many other signs in the presence of his disciples, which are not recorded in this book."
>
> John 20:30

The coin was simple and ordinary but displayed a powerful message. My Christian brother, Rob, had his pockets full of commemorative coins at a recent Men's Ministry event. He handed one to each of the many men gathered. On one side of the coin were engraved hands clasped in prayer. The other side featured the inscription:

> "I said a prayer for you today. I know God must have heard. I felt the answer in my heart, although He spoke no word."

I took the coin, said thanks to Rob, and slipped it into my pocket. The gesture and coin were nearly forgotten until I encountered Charles later that evening. Charles is my neighbor. He and I have developed a nice friendship, and he has openly shared his story. I had told him that I wasn't concerned about his checkered past or that he sported a long ponytail or that he was unemployed, or that he had been to prison. He seemed to appreciate my respect for him. Charles has lived a rough, difficult life, but he is a great guy with a big heart. He told me he believed in God and that he prayed over his meals. That has been the extent of our spiritual connection.

Christian brothers in our Men's Ministry and I have been praying for Charles for quite some time. During our routine backyard chat, I impulsively reached for the coin, gave it to Charles, and told him it was a gift. Charles carefully examined the praying hands and slowly read the prayer on the reverse side. After a long pause, Charles looked at me with a tear in his eye and said, "Why would you do such a thing? And today of all days. You don't know, but my mother died yesterday." After regaining his composure, Charles said, "Thank you, I needed this. I will surely keep this coin." He left for his house with tears in his eyes.

Jesus performed many miracles during His life—many more than were recorded. I believe He still performs them today through His Holy Spirit. From Rob to the Men's Ministry to Dave and right to Charles' heart—the coin has found its perfect home. The coin was simple and ordinary but displayed a powerful message.

Treasures in Heaven

Matthew 6:19-21

I lost it all. Twenty-six years ago, while moving from one city to another, thieves broke into my storage unit and stole everything I owned. Gone forever were my furniture, electronics, clothes, books, appliances, sports gear, framed portraits, and, well, everything. Perhaps the most gut-wrenching aspect was the loss of my personal items—everything from my baseball card collection to photographs to a lifetime of handwritten letters from my mother.

Losing everything was excruciatingly painful. I was left with only my car, a set of golf clubs, and a few clothes. As a bachelor, I had achieved my goal, over those years, of collecting all the "important" things in life—"for myself." Now, everything was gone. I was crushed. There ultimately would be no insurance settlement. Police investigations were futile. Consoling friends were of little comfort. Even my wise mother was speechless. Until she offered this scripture:

> "Do not store up for yourself treasures on earth where moth and rust destroy, and thieves break in and steal. But store up for yourself treasures in Heaven where moth and rust do not destroy,

> and thieves do not break in and steal. For where your treasure is, there your heart will be also."
>
> Matthew 6:19-21

That, indeed, caught my attention. But back in my new home city, I was still inconsolable. A friend suggested I attend a local Men's Prayer Breakfast. Having exhausted all other ideas, I reluctantly agreed to attend the breakfast being sponsored by a mega-church I had never attended. I sat quietly eating my pancakes in a room of over 200 men, where I knew no one. Then a man approached me, holding out a baseball cap. He saw my Bible on the table in front of me and said, "Son, I'm today's speaker. If you know how to read that Bible, then reach in this cap and grab a verse. When I call your verse, stand up and read it like the rest of the guys." As he left, I opened my crumpled Scripture verse and saw written on the randomly distributed note, Matthew 6:19–21.

My possessions were still gone forever, but the intensity of my spiritual journey had taken a giant leap forward. Over the years, I have regained possessions but not as many, and they no longer seem as important. I've now been an involved member of that church for nearly three decades and have witnessed Jesus do many nearly unbelievable things in the lives of countless people, including my own. I've heard incredible sermons and been involved in very meaningful volunteer projects. I have been a member and teacher of many amazing Bible groups. I have written over fifty published stories on the lives of the spiritually transformed.

Through it all, there was one constant, not me or my deeds or my possessions, but Jesus. I know of many scriptures. They all touch my heart, but none like Matthew 6:19.

Insults

> "Then they spit in his face and struck him with their fists. Others slapped him."
>
> Matthew 26:67

As a frequent writer for Christian publications, I have ample opportunity to share my published stories. Targets, in addition to standard readership, typically include family and Christian friends. These writings also find their way to a variety of blogs, apps, emails, and texts. I often receive praise and compliments.

That encouragement and notoriety feel good. I try to focus on the proper attitude, but humility can be elusive. I realize encouragement is good, but I also know that pride is stubborn. After pondering my heart and the best, most humble, use of these writings, I embarked on a totally different approach. I decided to send one of my Christian writings to every non-Believer or casual Christian that I could think of. With my newfound, enthusiastic, evangelical fervor, I gathered every email address target I could find. I attached the document and confidently hit the send button.

The feedback was varied. Several were complementary,

but many did not respond. One response, in a reply to all, said, "Yeah, right, I remember when we got drunk together in college." The most vicious reply, to a group of twenty or so, said, "HINKLE, WHY DON'T YOU SHUT UP AND STOP PROMOTING YOURSELF!" I'd like to say I shrugged that off. But I didn't. I was angry and upset. I was ready to respond and set the record straight. The guy, who I know, deserved a tongue lashing, and I was about to administer it. But I resisted. I'm not sure how. Maybe it was the memory of Matthew 27:14 when facing false accusations before Pilate, we learned, "Jesus made no reply."

The next morning, I was very grateful for my silence. But, throughout the day, Jesus kept nagging at me. I thought of the insults hurled at Him. I thought of Him being mocked and spit upon. I thought of those who betrayed Him. I thought of the shame and humiliation he endured. I thought of His pain and suffering. I thought of an unspeakable crucifixion. I thought of how He remained silent and never unleashed His mighty power. I thought that He did it for even me. Then I thought of that tiny little insult I had received. I was crushed, moved, ashamed, amazed, and deeply grateful all at the same time. Perspective is everything.

All I Really Need

> "Do not be like them, for your Father knows what you need before you ask him."
>
> Matthew 6:8

I laid aside the devotion titled "All You Need Is Jesus" and stared at my new flat-screen television. The silent black thing stared back at me. The remote control was confusing as I had not used one in nearly a year. I managed to turn on the TV, and I heard something about a filibuster. Then I turned it off. My mind went back to 1965, my first memory of television. Our family television received three black and white channels: ABC, NBC, and CBS. The set probably weighed 500 pounds and was perched on a rickety stand. I was the remote control, meaning I sat nearest the television and adjusted the dials per Dad's direction. If we turned the rabbit ears just right, we could receive a snowy version of public television. How exciting!

More exciting was the world we learned about through that RCA wonder. "Gomer Pyle," "Andy Griffith," "Bonanza," and "The Brady Bunch" were on in prime time, and we never missed an episode. The only disappointing aspect of that TV was how it mocked me on Sunday and Wednesday nights. No "Wonderful World of Disney" or "Wizard of Oz" for me because they always aired on Sunday church nights. Walter Cronkite taught us all about Vietnam, Apollo 13, Watergate, Martin Luther King Jr., and John F. Kennedy. I fell in love with Cher and "I Dream of Jeannie." I eagerly awaited the Saturday game of the week, the only game on television that week. That television opened this country boy's eyes to a big world.

I've since seen televisions with 500 channels, but I have never enjoyed TV more than I did in 1965. Where did my joy go? Early last year, I gave up television, but not for any spiritual reason. I just lost interest. I've had cable for many years, but the number of channels that kept my interest kept reducing until there were none. Even sports, politics, and news had become quite predictable and monotonous. So, I turned off the TV. I've learned a lot since forsaking television. I rediscovered reading and silence. I read the Bible more. That turned out to be a good thing. The remote was no longer in control. Yes, I watched television when visiting folks, but I grew to enjoy the quiet of living without a television.

But at this moment, I was not interested in silence, watching my new television, or reading my Bible. So, I went out for chicken wings and, for some reason, began counting the televisions mounted on the walls. There were twenty-nine. Most people, including the staff, were staring at the televisions or at their phones. I felt older because I remember when restaurants did not have televisions, so I left.

I got in my SUV, turned on my GPS, then drove aimlessly, thinking about abbreviations, HBO, CNN, ESPN, UPS, 401k, DVR, BCS, ATF, SEC, ATV, NFL, FBI, PGA, CSI, FedEx, SARS, AARP, and IBM. Where did all these letters come from? Are we in too big of a hurry to pronounce words correctly? Abbreviations are certainly not new (see BC/AD), but the bombardment of them is bordering on ridiculous. I'm starting to believe we have too much stuff, too many gadgets, too many abbreviations, and we're too busy. Maybe I am getting wiser. Maybe I am getting older and crankier.

I returned home and began staring at the blank flat screen again. The brand name is LG. What does that mean? Why had I bought this? Maybe it was because I was the only one that didn't have one. Maybe it was because the teenage salesman was smarter than me. I do know that he laughed because I did not know the difference between LCD and LED.

Maybe I bought the television because my college-aged nephew was coming for a visit. Maybe it was because my eighty-two-year-old mother has a flat screen. Maybe it was because March Madness was pending. Why was I so ambivalent about what should have been an exciting purchase? I don't believe it was an especially spiritual thing because, after all, my old television idol was, in fact, replaced by my laptop idol.

I'm not sure if I can live without Wi-Fi. Plus, I just got new apps and iTunes for my iPhone. I text and e-mail like crazy. I spend hours in front of non-television screens. No super saint here. I turned on my new television and heard something about a kidnapping in California. I turned the television off. I reached for my laptop and turned it off as well. I silenced my phone. I thought about my grandpas and the limited role technology played in their lives. I thought for a moment about stuff, gadgets, technology, and how fast this life is moving. Then, in the stillness, I reached for my devotional book. It was still turned to the page, "All You Need Is Jesus."

Peculiar People

> "But ye are a chosen generation, a royal priesthood, an holy nation, a peculiar people; that ye should shew forth the praises of him who hath called you out of darkness into his marvelous light."
>
> 1 Peter 2:9

Working from home during the COVID era brings some unique advantages. I have found that taking in the sights and sounds of the neighborhood from my living room windows can be most interesting in a way that I never observed before. One example is Jeffrey.

I first noticed young Jeffrey attempting to dribble a basketball down the street. The ball seemed to be in control more than Jeffrey. His attempts to ride a bicycle were equally futile, as were his efforts with a baseball and glove. His lawn cutting performance was comical. Jeffrey's clothes were unusual. He even looked peculiar. I found myself observing Jeffrey more than my work.

I know his name is Jeffrey only because one day he knocked on my door. When I opened the door, Jeffrey stared at me, speechless. I asked him what he wanted, but he remained silent. I told him my name was Dave, and he said his name was Jeffrey but that he had forgotten what he wanted to say. I told him that if he remembered to come back. He left like a jet. Observing Jeffrey, on occasion, became a welcomed diversion from my laptop and iPhone. Jeffrey was better than a Zoom. I thought of Jeffrey a lot. Maybe more than I should. Usually, his antics brought me a smile and a chuckle.

Perhaps it's an unfair judgment, but Jeffrey is odd. He is unusual. He is peculiar. He is a strange little fellow. I'm glad I'm not like Jeffery. Glad until I found myself preparing to lead a Bible class on 1 Peter. In a few short verses, Peter admonished the first century Christians to be unusual people, to be strange, to be peculiar, and to be aliens. Peter, of course, was encouraging his fellow Christians to be distinctive, different, and set apart from the carnal people they lived amongst. By being distinctive, the Christians could attract them to the one they followed—Jesus Christ.

Centuries later, we are called to do the same. Maybe we don't have to wear unusual clothes or fumble a basketball, but we are called to live distinctive and holy lives, biblical lives, and Christ-like lives that attract others to Him. My epiphany of sorts led me to re-think Jeffrey. Maybe he has a disability. Maybe he has no father. Maybe I should get to know his family. Maybe I could teach Jeffrey how to ride a bicycle or dribble a basketball. Maybe, just maybe, they need to see someone distinctive. Maybe I can be odd, strange, unusual, and peculiar in a Christ-like way. Maybe by so doing, I can make a difference in someone's life—someone like Jeffrey.

Trust

"Offer the sacrifices of the righteous
and trust in the Lord."

Psalm 4:5

I truly enjoy high school class reunions. I love the old stories and all the laughs. Most of all, I love seeing and learning about the transformation over the years of my classmates. One such case was Richard. Richard and I, both from large, meager-income families, worked together, sacking groceries at Whipple's Food Market in rural Western Kentucky. We developed a nice friendship, but our high school experiences were quite different. I was President of the Student Council and quarterback of the football team. I was also a fun-loving, often full-of-myself, troublemaking prankster. I was generally what we classified in those days as "popular." Richard, though well-liked and respected, was quiet and mostly kept to himself.

At this reunion, I was doing what I typically did—scanning the room, searching for my next conversation target. And that is how I spotted and then immediately engaged Richard. I had not seen him since high school.

He looked different. For starters, he was wearing a neat suit—not flashy or stuffy—just impressive. Far beyond appearance, he displayed appealing traits. He had a wide, friendly smile. He was gentle, peaceful, calm, and well-spoken. He was confident yet humble and had piercing, focused eyes that looked right through me. He made a strong first impression. We didn't talk much about the old days. But we did end up talking about Jesus, the Holy Spirit, His Word, and His church—The Resurrection Kingdom Center, where Richard is their pastor. I left that evening thinking that I had experienced, through Richard, the fruit of the Spirit—love, joy, peace, patience, kindness, goodness, faithfulness, gentleness, and self-control. I also thought that Richard should have been voted high school "Most Likely to Succeed" and certainly, "popular" in the kingdom.

Much time went by until I somehow found myself across a breakfast table from Richard. We were discussing how to successfully deal with life's challenges when he drew, on a napkin, an illustration of a technique he used. It goes something like this. Draw a blank line ________________________ followed by the words, "nevertheless, I trust You." Richard explained further that any problem could be written on the blank line—as many problems as you choose, as often as you like. Repeat the completed phrase over and over until you believe it.

The word "trust" is mentioned nineteen times in the Bible, most in powerful promises. Perhaps the most popular is Proverbs 3:5, "Trust in the Lord with all your heart and lean not on your own understanding; in all your ways acknowledge Him, and He will make your paths straight." My personal favorite is Psalm 32:10, "The Lord's unfailing love surrounds the man who trusts in Him." Like you, I have faced many intense challenges in life. Scripture never fails to comfort and guide, but perhaps the blank line technique has helped me the most. Thanks, Richard.

____

nevertheless, I trust Him.

Chains

> "And because of my chains, most of the brothers and sisters have become confident in the Lord and dare, all the more, to proclaim the gospel without fear."
>
> Philippians 1:14

I've often heard said, "He (or she) led them to Christ." I suppose it's possible for one person to lead another to Christ, but that has not been my experience or observation. The image that comes to mind is a chain connecting a person to Christ, with many people forming the links in that chain.

Consider the case of Dan. Dan was greatly impacted by the loss, in high school, of his mother, Doris, to cancer. Her last request of Dan was that he be baptized. Though he loved his mother with all his heart, he declined. Dan said he always regretted that decision. In college, Dan may have been the most popular guy on campus. I know because I was his roommate as well as sidekick in the usual college antics that were far from spiritual. Dan was always smiling, laughing, engaging, funny, and quite the favorite of all. As a mutual friend once said, "To know Dan is to love and laugh."

Many years after college, Dan and I enjoyed a great dinner together. I noticed that his conversation was sprinkled with words like "Christ," Holy Spirit," "The Word," and more. He had that same effervescent and passionate spirit but now, with a different twist. That joy was apparent even as he shared some very serious challenges in his life. My curiosity got the best of me, and so I asked him, "What has gotten into you with this new spiritual angle?" Dan recounted events of the past few years, the people who had impacted him, and the freedom he discovered in Christ. Recognizing a good story, I went in search of these people.

John, a Christian and Dan's neighbor, had developed a special bond with Dan. They spent many hours on the front porch, discussing life and spiritual matters. One of Dan's co-workers, Chris, took a special interest in Dan. Chris, over quite some time, stayed focused on planting Christ-like seeds in Dan. When Chris needed support in his efforts, he turned to co-worker Rick, who also encouraged Dan. The co-conspirators led Dan to a weekly Bible study at Southeast Christian Church in their hometown of Louisville, KY. Over the course of many months, Dan was an enthusiastic participant. A new link connected Dan with Mike, Senior Minister of Hurstbourne Christian Church in Louisville.

Mike and Dan, two very similar strong personalities, sparked an intense friendship that continues today. Ultimately, Mike baptized Dan, along with his wife and son, into Christ. Decades later, the last wish of Doris was fulfilled. Today, Dan serves as a senior church leader. He leads mission trips and works with the youth of the church. He is responsible for leading many key church ministries. His regular seat at church is rarely empty. More importantly, the effervescent, funny, smiling, laughing, encouraging, compassionate, humble, caring, intelligent, infectious, vivacious person that is Dan is still a magnet—now a magnet for Christ. So, from Doris to John to Chris to Rick to Southeast Christian Church to Mike to Hurstbourne Christian Church, and likely many others, the links of the Holy Spirit served their intended purpose well and formed a strong chain—connecting Dan firmly to Jesus.

Encouragement

"Therefore, encourage one another and build each other up, just as in fact you are doing."

1 Thessalonians 5:11

The Bible is very clear on encouragement. Scripture offers many examples. Moses encouraged Joshua. David encouraged Joab. Job (of all people) encouraged his friends. Barnabas' name means "Son of Encourager." The Apostle Paul, who suffered intensely, was also an encourager. He writes the word "encourage" thirty-two times in the New Testament as he continually encourages the first-century churches. Jesus was the ultimate encourager and is even encouraging us today through the Holy Spirit.

How does encouragement work today? Sometimes it is soothing and comforting. But also, as with Jesus, encouragement can be sharp and to the point, like one instance in the most brutal phase of my life. Ten years ago, I lost almost everything—my wife through divorce, my young children to a faraway state, my father, one of my best friends, my health, my money, my house, my job, my career, and even my dog. For weeks, I sank into deep depression, did not work, took little food, and lived mostly in bed. Then came encouragement in a most unusual form.

A life-long close friend and brother in Christ visited me. He sat beside me and offered these simple words, "Are you going to give up?" I let the words soak in. At first, I was irritated because he offered no sympathy. But then the words of Jesus also came to mind. "Do you want to get well?" So, I promised my friend I would not give up, and I thanked him. He said, "That's all I needed to hear." Shortly thereafter, he left. No pity, no speeches—just a simple question that struck me in the heart and still does today. His odd form of encouragement made a world of difference.

Thanks to him and the encouragement of many others, as well as the grace of God, I have mostly recovered. So, I now, with sympathy or a challenge, try to encourage all I encounter. May these words encourage you, and may you encourage those around you. You'll be glad you did. They will be glad. And so will your Heavenly Father.

Put on the Full Armor of God

Ephesians 6:10–18

As a boy running out the back door, I still remember Mom sternly saying, "Put on your coat!" I thought she was crazy. Maybe she was worried about me catching a cold or being frostbitten. Maybe the coat made a difference, or maybe not. Maybe it was just to make Mom feel better. I'm not sure, but I do know that I always ended up with the coat on.

As I advanced to a more mature age, my outerwear became more sophisticated—and expensive! Wool socks, leather boots, fleece jackets, thermal gloves, and headbands did the trick—especially when they featured fancy brand labels. Mom and Dad couldn't afford such, but I found a way to stay warm and, more importantly, a way to impress the girls!

As "the girls" turned into a wife and children, these clothes became more critically important. They provided warmth for outdoor winter chores and to escape, for a while, my noisy family. But "critically important" more aptly applied to my buddies who joined the military.

My friend, Rob, served as a U.S. Army Ranger for several years. His gear required for warfare included multiple weapons, camouflage clothing, a load-bearing equipment belt, ammunition rounds, a bayonet, field bandages, a canteen, lighters, burlap suits for disguise, waterproof boots, bulletproof helmets, and more. Evidently, danger and death were possibilities. Freedom and life were at stake. But now, my comrade, Rob, wisely embraces the full armor of God.

The Apostle Paul instructs us to put on the belt of truth, the breastplate of righteousness, the shield of faith, the helmet of salvation, and the sword of the Spirit (Ephesians 6:14–17). Why are these so critically important? Paul explains:

> "Put on the full armor of God. So, you can take your stand against the devil's schemes. For our struggle is not against flesh and blood but against the rulers, against the authorities, against the powers of this dark world and against the spiritual forces of this dark world and against the spiritual forces of evil in the heavenly realms."
>
> Ephesians 6:11-12

Danger and death are possibilities. Freedom and life are at stake. As for me, I've graduated from a simple coat to sophisticated outerwear to the full armor of God. Mom was not crazy after all. Today I daily put on that armor. Mom, a major spiritual influence in my life and a dedicated life-long Christ follower, looks down from heaven and reminds me. "Put your coat on! And, put on the full armor of God!"

The Tongue

> "The words of the reckless pierce like swords,
> but the tongue of the wise brings healing."
>
> Proverbs 12:18

The tongue may be a small part of the body, but the Bible has big things to say about speech. Scripture includes 129 references to the tongue, mouth, lips, and our words—most of them in the context of warnings. To name a few—"No man can tame the tongue. It is a restless evil, full of deadly poison." (James 3:8). "A gentle answer turns away wrath, but a harsh word stirs up anger." (Proverbs 15:1). "When words are many, sin is not absent, but he who holds his tongue is wise." (Proverbs 10:19). "The tongue has the power of life and death." (Proverbs 18:21). Perhaps I could write several pages on those references, but I won't preach a sermon here.

I will just offer a simple illustration of the power of a reckless tongue. Recently, I was preparing to lead our small group Bible study on the subject of "The Tongue: Life & Death Words." Halfway through my preparation, I decided I needed a donut. (A delicious, unhealthy craving of mine!). So, naturally, I drove to my favorite donut shop.

It's my favorite because they have a drive-thru window, and the friendly ladies know me by name. (I go there way too often.) They fix my coffee just the special way I like it. Then they give me a free donut! See why I go back?

Unfortunately, on this day, I was greeted by a new face. No problem, I would explain the long-held routine. The young man responded, "I can't do that." No problem, I would explain the routine in clearer terms—after all, I am well trained in persuasive salesmanship. This time he responded, "I can't do that." I asked if the friendly ladies were there. "No." So, for the third time, I explained. He responded, "I can't do that. I would get fired." So, I did what any fine, upstanding Christian teacher would do (not). I pointed my finger at him and said in a forceful voice—"You SHOULD be fired! This is ridiculous!" And I drove away.

Back at the house, coffee and donut-less, I decided to bury myself in Bible study until I looked at the study title—"The Tongue—Life & Death." Great. Conviction and no sugar or caffeine. I wrestled with my conscious and guilt until driving back to apologize. The young man was gracious, but the damage could not be totally erased. You can't "unsay" some things.

Perhaps this was a minor mistake, impulsive behavior,

reckless use of the tongue, just plain sin, or all. My behavior certainly was shameful and embarrassing. Maybe this is a simplistic illustration (I've done worse), or maybe not. What I do know is that I was wrong. I know that words can sting. I know that words can hurt. I know that words cannot easily be forgotten or forgiven. And I know that it's unlikely I will have a conversation with that young man about Jesus.

Carrying Crosses

"Then he said to them all: "Whoever wants to be my disciple must deny themselves and take up their cross daily and follow me."

Luke 9:23

It may have been the perfect Sunday. The members had begun streaming into the small country church just like they did weekly, but this day was different. The crosses they wore were visible. Some crosses were small, fitting neatly on a lapel. Others were so large the bearer was nearly crushed under the weight upon their back. The crosses were wooden or steel, heavy or light, depending mostly upon the attitude of the carrier. Some crosses were new while others were weathered, having been drugged for years. Many tried to act as if they had no cross at all, even though it was plainly there.

Despite the unusual scene, everyone acted as if nothing were different. Irrelevant small talk was common among the cross-bearers. Most preferred to talk of the weather instead of the obnoxiously large crosses. Many bore crosses for which they shared no blame. Some created their own cross while preferring to blame others. Many took pride in their cross, telling a tale to all who would listen. Some helped others with their cross, but most were too focused on their own cross. Almost everyone was more concerned about their clothing than the cross on their back. An elderly woman slowly entered the church with a cross so aged that it appeared embedded in her back. Next to her was a teen—her cross new but equally heavy. Families arrived together, each with their own cross. Everyone had a cross—except for the little children.

Some carried their crosses with dignity, others with shame. A few crosses were so incredibly heavy that the persistence of their owners was inspiring. Other crosses were feathery, in comparison, but not to the owner. Smiles were on the faces of some bearing a cross, but others showed fear, fatigue, and depression. Some had perfected, through experience, smooth navigation with their cross. Others could barely get to their seats. Some were looking for relief from their cross; others pretended they had no cross.

The service began just as it had every Sunday for the past hundred years. They sang memorized songs of joy and thanks. They repeatedly stood and sat, despite the crosses on their backs. They followed their rituals and obeyed their unwritten rules. Some sang with joy, while others went through the motions. Some prayed with hope, while others accepted their cross as if a life sentence.

The minister arose at the appointed time and made his way to the same place he stood every Sunday at this hour. No one seemed to notice or care that he, too, bore a cross of sin and shame. His message had meaning, for he had prepared at length. He had learned long ago that though his sermons might have little impact, life was easier without the guilt of making little effort. His words were like arrows shot aimlessly at the crowd. A few found the mark, but most fell harmlessly. Near the expected time, he uttered a familiar phrase that indicated he was near the finish.

The congregation automatically stirred in anticipation of an end. The minister closed with a final scripture, Matthew 11:28, "Come to me, all you who are weary and burdened and I will give you rest. Take my yoke upon you and learn from me, for I am gentle and humble in heart, and you will find rest for your souls. For my yoke is easy and my burden is light." The congregation rose and sang a familiar song of old. The minister stood alone, facing the congregation, trying to appear ministerial while the cross of failure on his back gained another five pounds. Then from out of the blue came a little man.

He slowly but steadily made his way to the front of the sanctuary. The now excited minister stepped to greet him, but the octogenarian just ambled right by. He stopped at the foot of the cross on the stage and stared up as if someone were there. The congregation continued to sing because there was nothing else to do. All eyes were on the little man as he reached over his shoulder, grabbed his cross, and dropped it at the foot of the cross in front of him. The singing stopped. The air was silent and thick. The little man dropped to his knees and wept with joy. A woman stepped forward and dropped her cross on top of his. Then a group of teens rushed forward and excitedly tossed their crosses on top of the two.

People began streaming down the aisles, eager to get rid of their crosses. Some knelt in praise; others jumped for joy. Some ran back up the aisle to help those dragging their crosses. But most didn't need help because the crosses suddenly seemed lighter. The pile of crosses dominated the stage. The crowd of cross-free people was singing and dancing. Soon, the only people left in their seats were those who had insisted they had no cross. But they, too, could ultimately not resist. Eventually, the seats were empty, and everyone celebrated around the pile of crosses at the foot of the cross.

Not a thought was being given to lunch or the time or Sunday afternoon plans. The mood was festive and joyful. Each rejoiced in their own special way, but each heard the same voice that spoke to their heart as the service ended. “That was nice. Let’s do it again tomorrow.” It was, indeed, the perfect Sunday.

Love Your Neighbor as Yourself

"The second (commandment) is like it:
'Love your neighbor as yourself.'"

Matthew 22:39

Two weeks before Christmas, my friend Justin and I were dining at our favorite restaurant. As the server, Monica, delivered our food, Justin informed her that we liked to pray over our food and wondered if there was anything we could pray for her. Monica did not hesitate as she said that she, her husband, and four children were living in a small hotel room and hoping to find a way to get a house for their family. We asked her if she would like to join us in prayer. She bowed her head. Justin prayed with sincerity, humility, and likely a lump in his throat. Monica left the table in tears. I must confess that I rarely give much consideration to servers. I am focused on my food! Given the circumstances, I did leave a generous tip, but even in this poignant moment, I quickly moved on.

Though my heart went out to Monica and her family, I really didn't know what else to do. I am not a wealthy man. Neither is Justin. The next day, I left town for the weekend, probably only thinking of my next meal, but Justin was inspired. He boldly approached two men's Bible groups we are members of. He passionately pleaded Monica's case. In short order, over one thousand dollars were gathered. Justin returned to the restaurant in a few days and presented the gift to a stunned Monica. The cash gift was enclosed in an envelope with these simple words written on the front, "From Jesus." Justin quickly left with no ado.

I returned to the restaurant a few weeks later and spoke with Monica. She said she was able to buy Christmas gifts for her children, pay off some debt and save money for a down payment on a house. She said she and her husband had never heard of anyone doing such a thing. She went back to work with tears in her eyes. I could comment for paragraphs on this most remarkable story. But I won't. The story and scripture speak for themselves.

The Cardinal

> "Can any one of you by worrying add a single hour to your life."
>
> Matthew 6:27

I often find myself gazing out a window and pondering some aspect of life. Unfortunately, I all too often am pondering problems, as was the case on this day. Lush green grass, a lovely neighborhood, and a gorgeous blue sky were right in front of my eyes, but my attention was focused on the all too familiar daily challenges—children, work, health, deadlines, bills, and a hundred other issues swirling rapidly through my mind. You know the drill. Then, seemingly out of nowhere, appeared a mind-changer. Hopping across the lawn was a gorgeous, bright red Cardinal. The bird was small but had the swagger of an eagle. He was merrily chirping, hopping from place to place, gathering crumbs to eat, and seeking out puddles to splash in. The Cardinal seemed to not have a care in the world and was plenty pleased with his little life. In fact, with some imagination, I could hear the bird giggling and laughing.

My father was always a patient, astute bird watcher and likely would have spent significant time observing the bird and its habits. But not me. I have always had things to do and places to go. Besides, my sanity or manhood might come into question if I dwelt too long on a bird. But just about the time, my mind returned to "normal," bird thoughts came crashing into my mind. "That bird is having more fun than I am. That bird is not concerned—about anything. That bird has no house, car, 401k, or any other possession, but the bird is more peaceful and content and joyful than I am." I tried to shake off these most unusual thoughts and return to so-called "normal," but the Cardinal lessons were beginning to build a nest in my bird brain.

I told my sister the story, and she promptly sent me a text of a beautiful red Cardinal. The text told a broader story. According to legend, the Cardinal, with rich red color symbolic of Christ's shed Blood, is a messenger sent from God appearing in times of stress and despair to encourage hope and persistence. Now that is certainly not biblical, but it is a nice warm thought. A vastly better and more precisely biblical verse did occur to me just a few moments later:

> "Look at the birds of the air; they do not sow or reap or store away in barns, and yet your heavenly Father feeds them. Are you not much more valuable than they?"
>
> Matthew 6:26

I could preach a sermon... But I think Jesus just did.

The Dream

"To these four young men God gave knowledge and understanding of all kinds of literature and learning. And Daniel could understand visions and dreams of all kinds."

Daniel 1:17

Next to Revelation, the book of Daniel contains what may well be the most vivid biblical examples of Godly dreams, visions, and prophecy. Clearly, Daniel was greatly gifted by God. There is much we do not understand about his gifts or this most intriguing biblical text, but there are some obvious conclusions we can draw. Daniel had keen and unique insight. He alone could accurately interpret the dreams of many, such as the powerful King Nebuchadnezzar. His explanations could be complicated or simple. His words were often suggestions or sometimes dire warnings. His dreams and visions could be pleasant or terrifying. His interpretations sometimes placed him in grave danger. We also know that Daniel prayed extensively and always gave credit to God. Some believe the gist of Daniel's story is, "bow before God." Are there modern-day prophets who, like Daniel, can interpret dreams? I don't know. What I do know is that our God is big, all-powerful, and can do whatever He wants. I also know that there are many experiences that leave me wondering. Consider the dream of my trusted Christian friend, Richard. He clearly and specifically recounts his recent dream.

"I saw in my dream a 'Heavenly Office' with angels sitting behind a long desk. I was on earth, and I was 'casting my cares' on the Lord, according to 1 Peter 5:7. ('Cast all your anxiety on Him because He cares for you.') My cares appeared in that 'Heavenly Office,' all printed on pieces of paper—one care per page. I figured they couldn't be all my cares because there was an unending stream of papers moving across the desk like they were on a conveyor. It must have been the 'Care Department' for everyone in the Kingdom of God. But they were just mine. As the printed pages moved across the desk, one angel stood at the end of the desk and took each printed care and ran it through a huge shredder. One by one, those cares no longer existed. They didn't exist on earth because they were cast upon the Lord and they didn't exist in Heaven because God dealt with each situation as quickly as the shredder could shred them."

Richard shared his interpretation of the message. "As long as we hold on to our cares, they remain, whether real or imaginary. But when we truly cast them upon the Lord, the cares are forever eliminated." Richard certainly would never want to be called a Daniel or a Prophet. I agree. But I do wonder, sometimes, what God might be up to when He sends these powerful biblical messages through our dreams. I don't know about modern daydreams, visions, and prophets, but I do know that our God is big, all-powerful, and can do whatever He wants.

Blessings Crown the Head of the Righteous

"Blessings crown the head of the righteous, but violence overwhelms the mouth of the wicked."

Proverbs 10:6

Mom's favorite hymn was "Count Your Many Blessings." Written in 1897 by Johnson Oatman, the simplistic yet powerful lyrics are below:

When upon life's billows you are tempest-tossed,
When you are discouraged, thinking all is lost,
Count your many blessings, name them one by one,
And it will surprise you what the Lord has done.
Are you ever burdened with a load of care?
Does the cross seem heavy you are called to bear?

Count your many blessings, every doubt will fly,
And you will keep singing as the days go by.

So, amid the conflict whether great or small,
Do not be discouraged God is over all,
Count your many blessings, angels will attend,
Help and comfort get you to your journey's end.

Likely learned in her childhood, Mom sang this song and counted her blessings through eighty-nine years of living on this earth. Mom and Dad (also a blessings counter) were indeed blessed. They had fifty-nine fantastic years of marriage. They raised seven wonderful children and loved their seventeen grandchildren. They had a faithful, robust church life and many trusted Christian friends. They were highly respected in their community. They traveled together. They both had successful careers—often working multiple jobs. They worked hard, but they knew that ultimately, they were saved by grace. And they were.

But life's billows did indeed tempest toss. They battled many steep challenges—dealing with a critically injured son, financial hardship, medical dilemmas, caring for their aging parents, sheer fatigue, and a host of others. Yet, I rarely heard them complain. Their humor and humility remained intact throughout. Perhaps, they were singing that song? The most crushing blow for Mom was the death of Dad. Fifty-nine years of marriage just didn't seem enough. Dad's eighty-two years were not enough either.

Dad's memorial service was held on January 1, 2012. One week after that service, we were gathered around the breakfast table when I asked Mom if she was sure that she wanted to go, so soon, back to the church building where Dad's service was held. She replied, "Well, where do you think we're going?" At the church building, we all sat in our routine places, with the exception of one conspicuously empty seat. The song leader approached Mom, smiled, and said, "Mrs. Hinkle, today is your lucky day. You get to choose the first song. Now you think about it, and I'll be back." Mom firmly and immediately replied, "I don't need to think about it. Sing 'Count Your Many Blessings.'"

The Gospel—in Two Minutes

> "For I am not ashamed of the gospel, because it is the power of God that brings salvation to everyone who believes: first to the Jew, then to the Gentile."
>
> Romans 1:16

Since the beginning of time, there has been God and man. Man, in one way or another, has always been drawn to God. This is likely true because man was created in God's own image. The problem has always been that whatever effort man makes to get closer to God falls short. Man has tried sacrifice, giving, good works, prayer, living a good life, better behavior, and any number of seemingly worthwhile endeavors. But they all fall short of being with God. We know this is true because the Bible says all have sinned and fallen short of the glory of God. Every single person in the history of the world falls short. Even Billy Graham, Mother Teresa, and certainly you and I fall short because of sin.

So, this is tragic news for the world because the Bible teaches that the wages of sin are death. Or, to put things in more blunt terms—we are all destined for hell. But God, in His infinite mercy, provided us with an escape. Essentially, He built a free bridge from us to Him, a bridge in the shape of a cross. The cross of Jesus Christ. God invites us to put down our efforts, cross the free bridge through the one and only way, Jesus Christ, and accept His offer of salvation. By so doing, one can say they are saved, not because of anything they did or did not do, but because of what Jesus Christ did on the cross.

Perfect

"Being entirely without fault or defect- flawless."

Merriam-Webster Dictionary

Jesus was perfect. Perfect. Period. He never made a mistake. He was the only perfect human ever.

His actions were perfect. His directions were perfect. His words were perfect. His thoughts were perfect. His plans were perfect. His love was perfect. His ministry was perfect. His commands were perfect. His role was perfect. His focus was perfect. His message was perfect. His compassion was perfect. His demeanor was perfect. His rebukes were perfect. His anger was perfect. His timing was perfect. His prayer was perfect. His silence was perfect. His teaching was perfect. His power was perfect. His leadership was perfect. His humility was perfect. His instructions were perfect. His example was perfect. His lifestyle was perfect. His choices were perfect. His courage was perfect. His meekness was perfect. His persistence was perfect. His grace was perfect. His guidance was perfect. His solitude was perfect. His forgiveness was perfect. His listening was perfect. His endurance was perfect. His patience was perfect. His baptism was perfect.

His transfiguration was perfect. His warnings were perfect. His anguish was perfect. His comforting was perfect. His promises were perfect. His peace was perfect. His redemptive power was perfect. His pace was perfect. His understanding was perfect. His sinlessness was perfect. His vision for the future was perfect. His joy was perfect. His thanksgiving was perfect. His miracles were perfect. His instructions were perfect. His contentment was perfect. His parables were perfect. His friendship was perfect. His healing powers were perfect. His lineage was perfect. His kindness was perfect. His principles were perfect. His motives were perfect. His gentleness was perfect. His self-control was perfect. His faithfulness was perfect. His birth was perfect. His childhood was perfect. His appearances were perfect. His counsel was perfect. His explanations were perfect. His obedience was perfect. His loyalty was perfect. His prophecy was perfect. His plan was perfect. His resistance to temptation was perfect. His submission was perfect. His sacrifice was perfect. His crucifixion was perfect. His death was perfect. His burial was perfect. His resurrection was perfect. His ascension was perfect. His destiny was perfect. He was perfect—for thirty-three years and eternally beyond.

Jesus was entirely without fault or defect. He was flawless. He was perfect. I believe I need to follow a man like that.

Surrender

> "I want to know Christ—yes, to know the power of his resurrection and participation in his sufferings, becoming like him in his death."
>
> Philippians 3:10

No one likes to surrender. Yet, surrender happens. The South surrendered to the North to end the Civil War. Japan surrendered to the USA to end World War II. Albert Gore surrendered his election campaign to George W. Bush. Donald Trump ultimately surrendered to Joe Biden. Criminals often surrender to authorities. I surrendered to my older brother when he pinned me to the ground.

We do not surrender easily. Winston Churchill said, "Never give in, never give in, never, never, never, never." Battles, though, can't always be won. They are often lost. We don't like to surrender to our spouses or our children. Surrender feels like defeat, and defeat hurts our pride and ego. Surrender makes us feel like a loser. Surrender feels like loss. Surrender is embarrassing and humbling. We do not like to surrender.

But perhaps there is such a thing as good surrender. Consider the life of Jesus. He was the most powerful man in the history of the world (Acts 10:38). He will return in power and glory (2 Thessalonians 1:7). At any moment, He could have called on His Father for thousands of angels (Matthew 26:53). He healed the sick, He brought back the dead, and He performed miracles of all kinds.

Yet, He also surrendered. Really? Yes. Look at the last chapter of His life. Don't believe me, read for yourself (Matthew 26–28). He surrendered to Judas, the Roman soldiers, and the Roman officials. He surrendered to the angry, hostile mob and the executioners. He surrendered His will, and He surrendered to the will of His Father. And all of this without raising His voice or His hand. He surrendered all.

So, what are we to do? Are we to surrender as well? Maybe it was best said in this hymn, written in 1896 by Judson Van De Venter:

All to Jesus I surrender;
all to Him I freely give.
I will ever love and trust Him,
in His presence daily live.

All to Jesus I surrender;
humbly at His feet I bow,
Worldly pleasures all forsaken;
take me Jesus, take me now.

I surrender all, I surrender all,
All to thee my blessed Savior,
I surrender all.

Surrender? Maybe not such a bad idea after all.

Heaven and Hell

> "Do not be afraid of those who kill the body but cannot kill the soul. Rather, be afraid of the One who can destroy both soul and body in hell."
>
> Matthew 10:28

I recently had the pleasure of spending a weekend in a major city with my sister Cara and her boyfriend Tom. We took in the sights of the city, an adventure greatly enhanced by the knowledge of Tom, a native of the city. Tom was a great host. We dined at several great restaurants and even took in a major league baseball game. The best of all was time together. Cara and I are quite close and were appreciative of the ample time we had, along with Tom, for laughter and good conversation. The weekend was heaven.

The most memorable jaunt, for me, was "the walk." We (they) decided to take a long walk through the downtown area. I was not excited, to say the least, about this idea. Unfortunately, I am out of shape, overweight, and was suffering from a groin injury. I am a prideful, competitive man, so I faked a smile and began. With in-shape Tom leading the way, pointing out and explaining various historical sites, I began to hurt and fall back. My pride and competitiveness, though, kept me reasonably close to Tom, with Cara walking beside me—probably out of sheer sympathy. Did I mention it was ninety-five-degree weather?

Sweating profusely, I realized that each step we took was one step further from our vehicle—fifty miles behind us, or maybe three. Then came the greatest words of the weekend when Tom said, "I think we should take the bus back." I could not have been more relieved. We patiently waited until the bus pulled up curbside. The doors opened, and I could see empty seats. I felt the cold air-conditioning blowing on my smiling face. I was in heaven until I heard a firm voice over the loudspeaker. "No mask, no entry!" I was back in hell.

Pridefully limping the three miles back (they declined my Uber suggestion), the most meaningful thoughts of the weekend came. There is indeed a place called hell, but it is unspeakably worse than the tiny discomfort I experienced. And—hell is eternal. I hear that decades ago, preachers very often spoke of the reality of hell. Not so much anymore—not a great marketing strategy. The best approach is probably somewhere in the middle. Consider this biblical reference to hell.

> "This is what happens to those who live for the moment, who only look out for themselves. Death herds them like sheep, straight to hell. They disappear down the gullet of the grave. They waste away to nothing—nothing left but a marker in a cemetery."
>
> Psalm 49:13

That is not a cheery message. Neither is hell mentioned numerous times in the Bible. A denied bus ride in the middle of a splendid weekend is not hell—but it is a good reminder of the reality of hell and the awesome awareness of salvation thanks to Jesus Christ.

The Main Thing

> "For what we preach is not ourselves,
> but Jesus Christ as Lord, and ourselves as your servants for Jesus' sake."
>
> 2 Corinthians 4:5

For over forty years, Bob Russell, retired Senior Minister of Southeast Christian Church in Louisville, KY, frequently reminded the congregation to "keep the main thing, the main thing." He, of course, was urging folks to keep Jesus at the center of everything. Evidently, Southeast took that message to heart in everything, for decades, from details of worship services to host international conferences to sweeping the floor. Doing everything with excellence, and focusing on Jesus, has become a mainstay at Southeast, and the results have been amazing.

Legendary Christian writer, Oswald Chambers, took a similar approach. He constantly used phrases like, "keep the Cross at the center of everything" and, "if your preaching doesn't center on the Cross, you're ineffective and missing the point."

But keeping the main thing, the main thing is not limited to nationally prominent mega-churches or famous Christian writers. Take the case of Ron and Linda Sandefer, members of the much smaller and less famous Central Church of Christ in Paducah, KY. Ron and Linda know a thing or two about the main thing. They have been Christians for over sixty-five years, and they have been married for over fifty-nine years. They have been a model of servant leadership for decades. Ron was presiding over the Lord's table one Sunday morning several years ago, where I just happened to be in attendance. I remember it like it was yesterday.

At the appointed time, Ron strode purposefully down the center aisle and took his place at the podium. He paused, then looked straight at the congregation. His confidence, silver hair, and steely eyes drew attention, as did his demeanor—not grim, but all business. Then he began his brief but most powerful and eloquent remarks. With his permission, I paraphrase the gist, "Folks, when it comes to church, fellowship is a wonderful thing. Singing is fantastic. Prayer is vitally important. Good preaching is a must." But then, Ron took another long pause and, with even more conviction, said, "All those aspects of church are important but THIS, pointing to the communion emblems, is the MAIN THING. Nothing else matters without this."

Like you, I have heard hundreds of remarks from men presiding over communion at the Lord's table. Many were fantastic, but I really don't remember any—except Ron's. So, if I've learned anything from this, it would be that fellowship, song, prayer, and preaching are wonderful; Bob is great, Oswald is fantastic, Ron and Linda are inspiring. But Jesus Christ is and always will be—
The Main Thing.

The Force

> "I am the good shepherd; I know my sheep and my sheep know me."
>
> John 10:14

Recently, I met a man named Dan. Dan asked me what I liked to do, so I told him about my writings of spiritual insight and transformation. I told him that everyone has a story—including him. It turned out that Dan was quite talkative as he then explained, in great agonizing detail, his four near-death experiences. In my attempt to change the subject, I asked him what God had taught him through all this. Dan explained that he did not believe in "things of old" but that his life was changed by the Star Wars movies. Dan feels that "The Force" is with him, guiding and protecting him. I asked him about Jesus Christ. He said Jesus was one of many forms of "The Force." I asked Dan what he thought of the Bible, and he then explained that a teacher long ago helped him understand that the Bible was full of inaccuracies and could not be trusted. He said, "I'm no sheep. Don't force-feed me."

We talked for a good while then I explained to him the Gospel. He eagerly accepted and agreed to be immediately baptized. Dan now serves as a Christian missionary in Kenya.

Okay, the previous three sentences are total fiction, but I did get my new friend's contact information, and we agreed to meet again (though I don't really want to). I have no idea what I will say, but I am confident the Spirit will lead me. To be continued.

What Now?

"Since everything will be destroyed in this way, what kind of people ought you to be? You ought to live holy and godly lives."

2 Peter 3:11

Our fledgling medical device company was in chaos. Product shipments from Europe were significantly delayed, causing backorders at hospitals across the country. Many of the surgical devices that did finally arrive were flawed. Customer service was receiving a record number of calls, and many of those calls were not pleasant. Promises had been broken. Our surgeon customers and hospital personnel were not pleased. Young sales reps, like me, faced difficult days. Commission checks were dwindling rapidly. Many employees quit. Our once promising venture was showing glaring signs of disaster.

I eagerly awaited my monthly visit from our sales manager, Gene. I was going to let him have it. I rehearsed my long list of problems, complaints, and consequences. I even chose the shade tree where I would take him for "conversation." Yes, for the only time ever in my career,

I was taking my own manager to the proverbial shade tree. Gene listened silently and carefully to my polite but very forceful diatribe. When I finished, Gene looked me square in the eyes and simply said, "That's all true. What do we do now?" I was stunned—no excuses, no long explanations, and no rationalization. Just eight simple words. A life lesson for me was taking shape. I had a choice. Quit, or get back to work—with faith.

Corporate executive, entrepreneur, and author, Doug Cobb, recently visited the Crestwood Warriors—our twenty-five-member daily Zoom prayer and scripture discussion group. Doug overviewed his most insightful and well-written new book about end times prophecy—And Then the End will Come. He explained, using scripture, possibilities, certainties, likelihoods, opportunities, challenges, and unspeakable coming disaster for non-believers. His work featured well-researched details regarding the imminent return of Jesus Christ. I jumped at the first opportunity for questions and asked, "So, what do we do now?" Doug looked me square in the eye and quoted 2 Peter 3:11—"you are to live holy and Godly lives." I immediately thought of Gene. I had a choice. Quit, or get back to work—with faith.

Noah, Abraham, Isaac, Jacob, Joseph, Moses, Joshua,

David, the Disciples, Paul, Jesus Christ, and every other biblical person faced the same choice. So do we. Quit, or get back to work—with faith.

Love Your Brother

> "A new command I give you: Love one another. As I have loved you, so you must love one another."
>
> John 13:34

My older brother, Steve, at age seventeen, a superstar in every regard, as well a Christian, was critically injured in a horrific car accident that left him with a severe traumatic brain injury for life. Steve has lived a most difficult and challenging life. He, and those around him, have had to deal with his anger issues and frequent, costly mistakes throughout his life. He has left lifelong psychological scars on his parents, brothers, and sisters—all of whom still love him and have helped him regardless over the years.

Thankfully, at the age of sixty-six, Steve has calmed down significantly, but many issues remain. Though living somewhat independently and peacefully, he is an odd character in behavior and appearance. He has significant memory issues and still makes poor choices and decisions. He is incapable of managing his money; he lives on a monthly disability check and the charity of family.

But Steve has a heart of gold and loves to help people. Unfortunately, that, too, causes problems as nefarious "friends," preying on his generosity, inevitably show up at his door on the first of each month, knowing that Steve is an easy target for "donations." Steve runs out of money frequently and must be bailed out by family. Countless speeches, explanations, or warnings are a waste of time, given his poor memory.

Only two days after my most recent financial reminder, I visited Steve. He let it slip that he had given a "friend" some money. I somehow remained silent until we were seated at the restaurant booth. I felt my head was about to explode, and my blood pressure was sky-high. No longer able to contain myself, I began to lecture him about all the times these people had harmed him, all the times we had to bail him out of financial jams, and all the things we had done for him in his life—meals, gifts, cash, and groceries.

Steve did not take it well. He responded with irrational arguments and defensive nonsense, then rose from the booth and began yelling at me. As all the diners looked on, Steve said in a loud voice, "I DON'T WANT YOUR FOOD, I DON'T WANT YOUR GROCERIES, I DON'T WANT YOUR MONEY, AND I DON'T WANT YOU TO EVER COME BACK HERE AGAIN!!!!" He then stormed out of the diner.

My embarrassment was overwhelming, so I apologized to the diners, the manager, and the server. I thought about tracking Steve down, but he lived only a few blocks away, and his temper was too high. So, as I started the long drive home, I didn't know whether to scream or cry. I was sad about his condition. I was angry about his behavior and ungratefulness. Until I passed a church billboard that simply said, "Love them anyway."

The Way

> "Jesus answered, "I am the way and the truth and the life. No one comes to the Father except through me."
>
> John 14:6

I do not like finding my way in the dark. But I have no problem finding my way when driving; GPS takes care of that. As a man, I generally don't like someone telling or showing me the way because—well—I'm a man. I do like finding a way out. I do not like going way down deep in the water, but I do like the way to the beach. I did not like learning the way to do calculus, but I did like skipping class and making my way to the lake. Frank Sinatra sang, "I did it my way." Burger King wants you to have it your way.

So, what's the deal with the "way"? Webster's dictionary defines "way" as "a path for traveling along." Good or bad? I suppose it could be either, depending on the path. Christians follow the words of Jesus, like the above very familiar passage that sheds light on the ultimate meaning of the way. Why are we to believe this? Well, it's in the Bible, and Jesus said it in plain words. He referred to Himself as "The Way." That is enough for me. The scripture itself is mostly self-explanatory. Most focus, and rightfully so, on the key words: Jesus, Way, truth, life, and Father. My favorite focus is the word "the"—the Way, the truth, the life, and the Father. I'm no word expert, but I believe the word "the" explicitly indicates "only."

Sadly, many people and religions worldwide, even some Christians, believe in multiple ways to the Father. One fellow, in all sincerity, explained to me that The Force from the Star Wars movies was the best way to God. Of course, many believe there is no way at all.

Let's face it; the above scripture is very bold. Jesus said that He is the only way to the Father. Because of that statement, there is no wiggle room and no other way. As many have said, Jesus was either a liar, lunatic, or Savior. We all must choose. I choose Savior.

Locked Out!

> "Then I will tell them plainly, 'I never knew you. Away from me, you evildoers!'"
>
> Matthew 7:23

For the past two years, during this COVID era, I, like many others, have worked from my home. With no office to go to daily and no business travel, there has been plenty of isolation, silence, and solitude. My best friend has been my laptop and its most appreciated feature, Zoom, where I can at least connect virtually with colleagues, family, and friends around the country. I cannot recall the vast number of Zoom calls I have been on, but there is one I wasn't on that I will never forget.

The Zoom invitation read, "Important Company Re-Organization Announcements." Not wanting to miss a second, I logged on early and then went outside for some fresh air. As I stepped onto the front porch and pulled the door shut behind me, I heard an ominous click. I had locked myself out of the house! The door would not budge, and the windows were sealed tight. I had no keys, no hidden key, no phone, no nothing—just empty pockets and a rapidly racing heart. Through a window, I could see my laptop screen displaying a blank wall where I was supposed to be. I could hear my phone ringing. I was firmly locked out. I do not like being locked out. Fortunately, a merciful, good Samaritan neighbor fetched a locksmith who arrived (one hour later) to let me in. I was so relieved. I was glad the Zoom announcements had not affected me, and my manager thought it was funny. There was, however, a huge takeaway.

In Matthew chapter 25, Jesus tells the parable of the Ten Virgins preparing for a wedding feast (the second coming of Christ). The five wise virgins had plenty of oil for their lamps, but the five foolish virgins did not. While the foolish virgins were away, gathering oil, the bridegroom (Christ) returned, and the door was locked shut. Despite their pleas, they were not allowed in. Jesus said, "Therefore keep watch, because you do not know the day or hour (of my return)."

In an even more terrifying parable (Matthew 25:41), Jesus said, "Then I will say to those on my left, depart from me, you who are cursed, into the eternal fire prepared for the devil and his angels."

"Hell" is no longer a frequent subject from our pulpits. "Hell" is clearly not a good church marketing strategy. Yet, Jesus mentions the horrors of "hell" fourteen specific times in the New Testament. Thank God that through accepting and following Jesus, we can escape the eternal fires of hell. I do not like being locked out. I do not like eternal fires.

Little Children

"And He said: 'Truly I tell you, unless you change and become like little children, you will never enter the kingdom of heaven.'"

Matthew 18:3

On my recent birthday, my wonderful sisters treated me to a picnic at Columbus-Belmont State Park. Most, even in Kentucky, have never heard of this little treasure tucked on the banks of the Mississippi River in the very far reaches of western Kentucky. The 156-acre site commemorates a Civil War encampment of Confederate soldiers preparing for a potential battle with Union troops. The park features preservation of that era, including historical placards, huge protective trenches dug by the Confederate soldiers, and a mimic of a giant iron anchor and chain used by the Confederates to span the river in an attempt to thwart the entry of the Union soldiers. Today, the park is also home to simple features such as picnic shelters, trails, and a small historical museum and gift shop.

After enjoying a great family lunch, I walked to the edge of the bluffs to take in the beautiful fall foliage overlooking the river. As I gazed back at the park, my memories returned to fifty years ago and the reason my sisters chose this site. This was where my parents took their children and friends for birthday picnics and days of relaxation. I could almost see myself and my ten-year-old friends, Terry Burns and Phil, running, playing, and laughing, exploring the park, climbing on the anchor, and enjoying grilled hot dogs, roasted marshmallows, birthday cake, and home-made ice cream. What a wonderful memory of a very simplistic time! I'm not sure that I have ever been as happy and joyful as I was then.

My mind returned to 2021, and I thought of modern-day family adventures like gigantic amusement parks and expensive vacations. What does all this have to do with a Christian inspirational devotion? Well, for me, I was also reminded that Jesus and his followers never enjoyed days at State Parks. They may have had enjoyable picnics by a lake, but they certainly never took in Disneyworld, Cancun, the World Series, or the Final Four. I've enjoyed some of those, and I thought of how expensive they are. My mind turned again to fifty years ago and remembered how happy and joyful I was with those days at the state park. Much more so than any glamorous weekend.

I think Jesus wants me to be that little child again.

Yes, He even said so. He is probably not interested in the stickers on my suitcase or car bumper, but I believe He is very interested in the joy of a heart released to Him like that of a little child. "God has hidden things from the wise and learned and revealed them to little children. Yes, Father, for this was your good pleasure" (Matt 11:25–26). "Let the little children come to me, and do not hinder them, for the kingdom of heaven belongs to them" (Matthew 19:14).

I think I need to go to Columbus-Belmont Park more often. I think I need to be more happy and joyful. I think I need to be more child-like.

Special Needs

"Do not judge, or you too will be judged."

Matthew 7:1

My eyes scanned the crowded coffee shop for an empty seat. I was in a rush to drink my coffee and catch up on emails, calls, and texts. I found one seat, just one. I approached the young man sitting in the adjacent seat and asked him if the seat had been taken. He never said a word and immediately turned his face away. I thought to myself, How rude! He must be one of those self-centered millennials who have no manners. Then I felt a tap on my shoulder. I turned to find a soft-spoken man who said, "I'm sorry, but that is my seat. I need to sit by Joshua. He is autistic."

According to the National Autism Society, autism is a genetic neurological disorder typically diagnosed in boys at the age of two or three. Autism impacts the normal development of the brain in the areas of social interaction, communication skills, and cognitive function. Individuals with autism typically have difficulties in verbal and non-verbal communication, social interactions, and leisure or play activities. One in fifty-four children in the U.S. is diagnosed with autism.

Matthew, Joshua's friend and caregiver, and I quickly engaged in a conversation. Matthew explained that Joshua is one of triplets. His brother is also autistic. Joshua's father died unexpectedly, and his mother is raising the three boys. Matthew, a highly successful business development executive, is also professionally trained in interacting with autistic children. On a weekly basis, Matthew takes Joshua out to the public for friendship, providing Joshua with much-needed exposure to social settings and giving Joshua's mother a bit of relief from full-time caring for three boys.

My heart was touched. My perspective had immediately changed. I was no longer in a hurry. My emails, calls, and texts could wait. I talked for a while longer with Matthew, who drew Joshua into the conversation. Before I left, with a tear in my eye, Joshua and I were smiling, laughing, and exchanging high fives. I had come for coffee and left with so much more.

I thought of the lessons I learned. I shouldn't be in such a hurry. After all, I don't recall a single biblical reference to Jesus being in a hurry. I don't recall Jesus not loving a special needs child (all of us). It's not about me, or my iPhone, or my emails, or my calls, or my texts. There is a lot going on around me that I need to be aware of. There are a lot of amazing people, like Matthew and Joshua's mother, doing amazing things. And most importantly, I need not be quickly judgmental—especially of Joshua.

We Can't Help Everyone, But We Can Help Someone

"The King will reply, 'Truly I tell you, whatever you did for one of the least of these brothers and sisters of mine, you did for me.'"

Matthew 25:40

In December of 2021, one of the most powerful tornadoes in the history of Kentucky ripped through Mayfield, KY, and surrounding areas. Lives were lost, homes and businesses destroyed. The city was decimated.

Loretta's business was in the direct path of the tornado yet, was nearly untouched—except for the now-gone fence that had been built to separate her business from some impoverished neighborhoods. Because of those neighborhoods, Loretta had never really liked the location of her business, but she surveyed the devastation in her part of town, said more prayers, then almost immediately devised a plan. She knew the needs were great and situations dire. So, Loretta went to work. The back porch of her business, near the demolished fence, was converted into a full-service kitchen to feed breakfast to the needy. Bacon, sausage, eggs, casseroles, fruit, coffee, and juice were served.

Word spread of Loretta's project, and donations and volunteers poured in, seemingly out of nowhere. A local church, its minister, and volunteer teams joined in. A farmer arrived with hundreds of eggs and then cooked them for four hours. Two dedicated ladies cooked bacon and sausage for four hours. Many volunteers brought food with them. One generous donor gave a very large storage unit that was converted into a storehouse of free donated goods for those in need—blankets, comforters, clothes, flashlights, batteries, and much more.

Word of free breakfast spread throughout the neighborhoods. Most of the people had no food. Some enjoyed their hot breakfast, then took platefuls home to others. One group of ten people, including children, were living in a damaged house with no heat, no electricity, little money, no job, and no car. Loretta and her team did the best they could to help.

Loretta mobilized a team to canvass the area in search of those who could not get out. Meals were delivered, and many other hungry folks were invited. Loretta's Team even began inviting other volunteers—utility workers, tree cutters, walking prayer warriors, and many others. Despite the dire circumstances, most everyone seemed to be in an upbeat, appreciative mood.

I'm not sure where all the money, food, and goods came from, but I suspect a good portion came from the pockets of Loretta and her hard-working husband, Mike. I also suspect that Jesus delivered in a big way—as He always does. Loretta believes she knows why that fence was blown away.

The Thief on the Cross

"Jesus answered him, 'Truly I tell you, today you will be with me in paradise.'"

Luke 23:43

Jackie was trouble and always had been. He was a trouble as a youth. He was a trouble as an adult—alcohol, drugs, children by multiple women, prison, and more. Worst of all, Jackie showed no signs of change. I never met Jackie, but I knew of him through his cousin, Derrick, who is an employee of mine. Derrick is a fine upstanding Christian family man and a highly respected professional who has enjoyed great success. Jackie and Derrick were very close. Jackie served as a pallbearer at the recent funerals of both of Derrick's parents. But Derrick's efforts to change the course of Jackie's life were futile. The efforts of many made no difference. Jackie was trouble and always had been.

But things finally changed for Jackie. With the help of a Christian woman Jackie had met and some caring Christian men, Jackie decided to change his life. Jackie dropped his bad habits, and he made amends to those he had harmed. He became a stand-up father and began attending church. Jackie even chose to become responsible and take on a legitimate job. He worked as a laborer, on the night shift, for a highway construction company. Derrick, his Christian brothers, and the Christian woman must have taken the advice of Winston Churchill, "Never give up, never, never, never." Jackie, against all odds, had indeed "put off the old and put on the new."

In the fall of 2021, at the age of thirty-seven, Jackie decided to be baptized into Christ. It was a momentous occasion. Jackie was finally at peace with Christ.

Two weeks later, while at work, Jackie was shot and killed in a random drive-by shooting.

A tragic ending and a somber reminder of the brevity of life as well as the urgency of salvation, but Jackie indeed got an early promotion to heaven and is thankfully enjoying his eternal reward.

Grandma Coffman

"But the eyes of the Lord are on those who fear him, on those whose hope is in his unfailing love."

Psalm 33:18

Mom was not without sin, but she was as close to sinless as I've ever seen. I heard her tell a lie once when she ran off a high school girlfriend of mine who she did not approve of. That's a little humorous now, but that is the only single lie I ever heard her speak in her eighty-six years of living. As a matter of fact, I don't recall any of her sins. As a favorite son, I realize my glasses might be a bit rose-colored, but the facts tend to speak for themselves. She was faithful to my father for fifty-nine years and to her church and her Jesus for a lifetime. She never drank, cursed, or smoked. I don't recall her ever gossiping, being envious, jealous, or hating anyone.

She loved the Lord her God with all her might, and she loved her neighbor as herself. She unfailingly loved her children. She may have broken one of the Ten Commandments, but I never saw it. Mom was full of humility and bulging with the fruit of the Spirit. I never heard a bad word said about her. She certainly wasn't perfect, but you get the point.

So, one day, I asked Mom why she was like that. Without batting an eye, she said, "Grandma Coffman." I had no idea who that was, but it was Mom's grandmother who cared for Mom as a child when her parents worked the farm (daily). Turns out, Grandma Coffman frequently told Mom, "He's watching you. All the time. He's watching you."

Mom said she was scared to do wrong. She said, to her dying day, that she always remembered that. Maybe Grandma Coffman was a fearmonger. Maybe not. I loved my Dad, and he loved me, but, as a boy, I feared him a little bit. That turned out to be a good thing. Most would agree that sometimes fear is a very helpful thing that keeps one from harm. Lessons I am learning here are to have a greater fear of God. Remember that the eyes of the Lord are always on me, and never underestimate the influence of a Godly grandparent.

I know these things not because I am wise but because the Bible tells me so. The phrase "fear God" is mentioned ninety-two times in the Bible—surely more than a mere suggestion. The phrase "eyes of the Lord" is mentioned 1one hundred and forty-six times in the Bible, so surely, He is watching—all the time.

I think Grandma Coffman was on to something.

Grandma Mary Penrod Coffman
1879–1956

The 'Thank You' Train

"But thanks be to God! He gives us the victory through our Lord Jesus Christ."

1 Corinthians 15:57

My friend and brother, Brian, loves to ride The Thank You Train. He told me that at one time in his life, he only prayed before eating and when in the midst of an emergency. He thought those few minutes were plenty, and he never thought a thing about it. Then, he decided he could do more, so he asked the Lord to teach him how to pray. Brian began pouring out all his troubles to the Lord. He said he felt better but thought there must be even more, so he began asking for things he wanted and praying over every aspect of his life, and asking for help in the major areas of his life—his health, business, plans, and finances.

Brian felt even better but had this nagging feeling that there was much more. So, he began praying for others. He prayed for his wife and children. He prayed, by name, for his extended family. As he continued to pray, the list grew longer and longer—friends, neighbors, co-workers, and many, many others. He began to take the "prayer list" from his men's group seriously, praying for people he didn't even know. He soon found himself praying for his church, his ministers, his country, and his President. He even mustered strength to pray for his enemies.

The amount of time Brian spent in prayer grew exponentially. He got up earlier. He stayed up later. But he found there were only so many hours in the day for solitary prayer, so he began to pray while in the shower, walking around, while driving, and even praying silently when in the company of others.

"That other prayer is great, but for me, I have to get on The Thank You Train. And stay there. I wake up, get on my knees, and say thanks. As I go throughout my day, I constantly, and usually silently, say thanks, over and over and over, thanks for Jesus, your Word, your Holy Spirit, your grace, mercy, and power. For my family, my job, my money, my friends, my health, even for adversity, and on and on and on. The list never stops. Sometimes the prayer goes on all day. I find my joy and perspective incredible when I am on The Thank You Train. It helps me when I visualize a very long train with Jesus as the conductor, my brothers and sisters in Christ on the train with me, and all of us smiling and praying thanks—all the way to heaven. Since getting on the train, I am so grateful and so joyful—no matter what. I'm staying on The Thank You Train.

Lamentations

"By their fruit you will recognize them. Do people pick grapes from thornbushes, or figs from thistles?"

Matthew 7:16

My father and I were very close. So, as he lay seriously ill in the hospital, the burden was heavy. Looking for comfort, one morning, I reached for my daily Bible reading—this day in Lamentations, chapter 3. Not exactly the uplifting, encouraging scripture I was looking for, but I read it anyway. The morose writings of the prophet Jeremiah made my soul sink even deeper with words like affliction, bitterness, hardship, darkness, and "my splendor is gone." I'm glad I kept reading because one word in verse 21 shifted my entire paradigm—"yet."

"Yet, this I call to mind and therefore I have hope:
Because of the Lord's great love, we are not consumed,
for his compassions never fail.
They are new every morning,
great is your faithfulness.
I say, the Lord is my portion:
therefore, I will wait on Him."

Lamentations 3:21-24

My father remained ill, but a load had been lifted from my shoulders. I left for coffee. On the elevator, I saw a couple I had never met before, but I was oddly attracted to them. I impulsively said, "You are believers, aren't you?" They smiled broadly, with a gleam in their eyes, and both said, "Yes, we are!" When we got off the elevator, we had a nice talk. I could tell right away that Henderson and Donna were wonderful Christian people. Henderson is a volunteer chaplain and was at the hospital to pray for a sick friend. I asked him if he would pray for my father. We agreed to meet in Dad's room in a few minutes.

As I got my coffee, thinking about this most unusual encounter, my mind turned to Galatians 5:22, "But the fruit of the Spirit is love, joy, peace, patience, kindness, goodness, faithfulness, gentleness, and self-control. I had recognized and encountered powerful fruit of the Holy Spirit!

Walking back into Dad's room, I discovered Henderson already there, praying. He was on his knees. His voice was soft, so I stepped closer to hear as Henderson prayed—Lamentations 3:21–24.

Your Next Assignment

> "Now an angel of the Lord said to Philip, 'Go south to the road—the desert road—that goes down from Jerusalem to Gaza.'"
>
> Acts 8:26

As mentioned in the Asa story, I once led a class entitled "Your Next Assignment." The purpose of our study was to better understand Philip's assignment in Acts Chapter 8 and its practical application to our lives today. As you know, Philip the Evangelist was preaching the Gospel with great success in Samaria. He performed many miracles and had such an impact that he was joined by Peter and John. Philip was evidently a biblical rock star of sorts, or perhaps the Billy Graham of his era. But an angel of the Lord told Philip to go to the desert in Gaza. Along the way, he met an Ethiopian eunuch, explained to him the Gospel, and baptized him. Many commentaries believe this eunuch was one of the first converts of Africa and thus a Gospel pioneer in that continent.

Our class concluded that God set in motion a most unusual set of circumstances. Philip had been preaching successfully to crowds; then, he was in the desert alone.

Philip's assignment was oddly timed, unusual, and likely uncomfortable. He left behind everyone and everything he knew. Philip, being human, was perhaps hesitant, if not reluctant, to go to, of all places, the desert. Yet Philip was obedient, and God had a much larger plan in mind.

In determining practical applications for us, we first noticed that this is often God's way of doing things. Abraham, Moses, David, Jesus Himself, Paul, and many others faced similar circumstances. Secondly, we concluded that for us today, our next assignment from God would also draw us out of our comfort zone, be unlikely, ill-timed, unusual, and uncomfortable.

We would likely be hesitant, if not reluctant. We might have to leave someone or something behind. The assignment might be to go to a faraway land or to go next door and speak with the neighbor we don't like. Finally, we agreed that the assignment might be coming, and we should be in preparation or that we already know exactly what the assignment is, and we just don't want to do it!

As the class was dismissed, I was approached by a woman I had never met before. With tears in her eyes, she handed me a small, crumpled piece of paper and told me to read it after she left. I did.

On the paper was written:

> "My assignment, if I chose to accept it, is to go visit the man who was convicted of the murder of my daughter. I have accepted."

I later met the woman and learned that she did, in fact, accept the assignment. Though the details of her story are quite personal, I know her words above are exact because the crumpled note is still taped to the inside cover of my Bible, some ten years later. It was the most dramatic display of obedience I have ever witnessed.

Jeff Lessons

> "Therefore, keep watch, because you do not know the day or the hour."
>
> Matthew 25:13

Jeff was one of my best high school friends and my hero in many ways. He lived in town where this farm boy would have many grand adventures with him. I spent many overnights at his home. His parents treated me like royalty. Jeff had a swimming pool and a putt-putt course in his backyard. He had a German Shepherd's best friend named Atlas. He could play the guitar. He was the first to get a car. Jeff was a great athlete and a great student. He was generous, kind, and humble. He had a great smile and a contagious laugh. The guys loved him. The girls loved him. I loved him.

Everything changed in May 1976 when Jeff, at the age of sixteen, was tragically killed in a car accident. Our small-town world was turned upside down. Everyone knew Jeff and his parents, and everyone loved them. We all were crushed. No one knew what to say or do. I would find solitary places and sob. I still remember sitting stunned in the funeral home as a man tried to explain to me how to be a pallbearer. I remember the new blue suit I was wearing.

Forty-six years later, I still think of Jeff. For some reason, I remember every May 14—his birthday. For several years, whenever I ran into his parents, none of us could speak. It was too hard. Life can be hard. Learning and experiencing that at age sixteen was excruciating. I have always thought that his death was one of the greatest injustices in the history of the world.

Somehow, life did go on, and somehow, a lot of positive processing did occur over the next 46 years because death teaches life lessons. I call them *Jeff Lessons*. There are probably more than a thousand, but I'll give you my top five.:

1. Salvation

I am grateful that Jeff's salvation was secure, but for many, my friend, Duck Commander Phil Robertson, says, "Doubt? Oh, you better get this one right with Jesus. Right now. It's your only way off this planet alive!"

2. A sense of urgency

Like Jeff, we never know. We're no more than one something, any moment, from the end.

3. SAY, "I LOVE YOU!"

4. Uncomfortable with hugs? Get over it! Please.

5. Go to funerals.

It's important. Pay your respects. You don't have to say anything; just be there. Maybe it was best said by Dietrich Bonhoeffer. "Time is short. Eternity is long. It is the time for decision."

I love you, Jeff. See you soon.

More Than a Miracle

> "Shortly before dawn Jesus went out to them, walking on the lake."
>
> Matthew 14:25

I am always amazed when an old, familiar passage takes on new life and teaches me something new. Such was the case with the story of Jesus walking on the water (Matthew 14:22–33). While reading Paul David Tripp's most excellent book, New Tender Mercies, I encountered the story again. In what most know from childhood, Jesus walks on water to rescue his disciples. The scripture is so familiar that I considered skipping on to the next chapter. I thought, Okay, I know this, the disciples were rowing merrily along when a storm came up. Jesus walked on the water and saved them from drowning. Got it. Yeah, I realize that Jesus is the only man in history to walk on water, but when reading the Gospels, miracles can become rather commonplace. I should have remembered that the living Word of God, sharper than any two-edged sword, is never commonplace.

The disciples were not rowing merrily along, singing kid's songs; Jesus had sent them across the Sea of Galilee, where they encountered an impossible headwind and very angry sea. Many commentaries agree that the disciples rowed for more than eight hours. In addition to being exhausted, they were in a situation that seemed impossible, frustrating, and dangerous. They did not have the strength or ability to continue. They must have been fearful, and surely it must have crossed their mind as to why Jesus had sent them there. Not exactly a funny joke. Another odd aspect of this predicament was that the disciples had not been disobedient. In fact, just the contrary—they were the good guys. But here, to me, is the most amazing aspect of the story.

Jesus could have prevented it all. With one prayer, one wave of the hand, or perhaps one thought, Jesus could have calmed the seas and rescued the disciples from peril. But He didn't. Why?

With the help of Matthew and Tripp, it dawned on me that Jesus needed the disciples to know they could really, truly, count on Him. How important would that be in what they would face in the months ahead? Most importantly, Jesus knew that the disciples needed locked-in proof that they needed a Savior, and Jesus was that Savior. The one who could—and would—and did, literally save them.

I thought about 2022. I thought about the power in

Jesus merely snapping His fingers. So, what about a terrible car accident? What about a child with cancer? What about a world war? And on and on and on. Why doesn't Jesus snap His fingers? Why does He not always intervene? I am no expert on Jesus' interventions, but I still believe that this lesson from Matthew 14 applies today. Yes, we live in a fallen world. Yes, sometimes He intervenes and sometimes not. Yes, He answers prayer or not. But I believe Jesus is more interested in hearts than events and outcomes. Just like the disciples, He wants us to be rock solid, sure that we can count on Him. And more importantly, He wants us to know deep in our hearts that we desperately need a Savior and that He is that Savior.

The Accidental Apostle

> "Since we live by the Spirit, let us keep in step with the Spirit."
>
> Galatians 5:2

As a former volunteer with the hospital visitation ministry of Southeast Christian Church in Louisville, KY, I frequently received interesting assignments. Usually, the call offered only a few details—hospital, patient name, room number, and maybe a few simple facts about the situation. My role was simple—introduce myself, listen, encourage, and offer a prayer. I enjoyed these adventures because there was a little mystery involved. People were appreciative, and each visit was different. Engaging with new people has always come easy for me, plus it's always good to help others.

On one assignment, I entered a room filled with friends and family members surrounding the bed of a man, either asleep or unconscious. From the serious tone in the room and the looks on their faces, I suspected the worst. I introduced myself and the purpose of my visit. They seemed quite receptive. They spoke in hushed tones about the man's condition. I gave them a few encouraging words and then offered to pray. I could tell by the look in their eyes that they were not accustomed to prayer. But I proceeded and noticed they were a bit uncomfortable when I asked if they wanted to hold hands. We all did.

I began praying, and after a short while, we heard a noise, and all looked up. The man was sitting straight up in bed and looking at me! I'm not sure how I regained my composure, but as the man lay back down and closed his eyes, I finished the prayer. The family stared at me with astonishment as if I were some sort of faith healer. We didn't talk much about it. I just left them with their thoughts. As I was leaving the room, I glanced up at the door placard. I had been in the wrong room!

After reflecting for a while, making sure I had the story straight in my head, I laughed out loud. I was in the exact room I was meant to be in. Something much bigger than me was in play. I began to ponder a few questions. What is Jesus up to in my world that I have no clue of? How many times has the Spirit used me and I had no idea? How powerful and all-encompassing is the Holy Spirit? How many times have I completely missed the Spirit? How can I stay more attuned to the Spirit? What does He want to do with me and a thousand other questions? The key question for me is what can I do to make myself more available?

The Holy Spirit is certainly far beyond my understanding but clearly worthy of my praise, gratitude, attention, and availability.

FINAL THOUGHTS

Mom and Dad nicknamed their seventeen grandchildren "The Peanuts." I'm not sure why, but we like it, and the name has stuck.

The Peanuts are compiling impressive credentials—a CEO, a marketing executive, a restaurant professional, an international language teacher and artist, a professor, an actor, an entrepreneur, two doctors, three ministry leaders, a triple degree graduate, a baseball all-star, a sports psychologist, a pediatric operating room nurse, a baseball stadium video specialist, a real estate agent, a child speech therapist, an attorney, a chef, an elementary educator, a master's student, and five more university under-graduate students.

They are spreading their wings throughout Kentucky, Illinois, the Middle East, Texas, Florida, Georgia, Virginia, Arkansas, Tennessee, South Carolina, Colorado, and Connecticut. Yes, impressive. So, Peanuts, don't stop! Go, Jennifer, Shane, Peyton, Lauren, Jonah, Erin, Salar, Maryam, Hassan, Ryan, Molly, Patrick, Olivia, Jackson, Emory, Asa, Heather, Bradley, Callen, Everett, Haley, Holly, Cody, Hannah, Camden, Nicolas, Christian and Ana Sofia!

CONCLUDING WORDS FROM JOHN

For the Peanuts—and all of us.

"I write these things to you who believe in the name of the Son of God so that you may know that you have eternal life."

1 John 5:13

ABOUT THE AUTHOR

Dave Hinkle, the father of three, is a businessman and an author.

CPSIA information can be obtained
at www.ICGtesting.com
Printed in the USA
LVHW081917010922
727261LV00009BA/446